EMBROIDERED BOXES

EMBROIDERED BOXES

Emma Broughton

CROWOOD

First published in 2019 by
The Crowood Press Ltd
Ramsbury, Marlborough
Wiltshire SN8 2HR

www.crowood.com

British Library Cataloguing-in-Publication Data
A catalogue record for this book is available from the British Library.

ISBN 978 1 78500 563 3

Frontispiece: close-up of the crewelwork embroidery
on the charm box from Chapter 4.

This book is dedicated to my mother, Janet Batten (1958–2015);
without her unfaltering belief this book would not have been possible.

Graphic design and typesetting by Peggy & Co. Design Inc.
Printed and bound in India by Parksons Graphics

⋅⋅⁂[CONTENTS]⁂⋅⋅

·ᵛᴬ[PREFACE]ᵃᵛ·

I have had a passion for boxes ever since I completed my large box project during my apprenticeship at the Royal School of Needlework. Although box-making has fallen out of fashion in recent years it is my aim with this book to bring it to the forefront of craft making. By using traditional techniques with contemporary designs and methods I hope that you will find constructing a box as fascinating and rewarding as I do. For me, embroidery (along with many other crafts) has been a lifelong love, starting with learning to make lace at the age of five.

I used to dream about spending all day stitching or working on other craft projects (probably from watching too many period dramas) and during my apprenticeship I was able to do so; now I am fortunate enough to have my own studio and the time to do just that. More and more people are now picking up the needle and are excited to learn the skills that I have gained during my apprenticeship and beyond, and it is a privilege to share my knowledge through teaching and by writing this book.

This guide will take you through the methods of box construction from basic to more advanced techniques in the form of projects with clear step-by-step illustrations and text, which can be adapted for your own use. I have provided illustrations for the stitches used in the embroideries and a working order; however, it was beyond the scope of this book to provide full step-by-step instructions for all the embroidery stitches due to the number of techniques I have used. Hints and tips have been included where necessary to help you in the construction of your box and stitching of the embroidery for it. I have also provided alternative design ideas in each of the chapters to help start you off on your box-making journey; I have included as many different variations as the scope of this book allows, but of course there are many more possibilities. Finally, I have included the suppliers from whom I purchase many of my materials, a stitch glossary, and a list defining more general terms.

I hope that the designs I have created will inspire you to create your own themed boxes, which can be a graceful or elaborate work of art and may even become an heirloom treasured by generations to come.

ABOUT THE AUTHOR

For as long as I can remember I have been practising one form of craft or another, whether it has been embroidery, painting, beading, quilting, patchwork, crochet or lace making; I usually have a project on the go, ready and waiting to be continued during any spare time. My mother was my most influential teacher; when I was growing up she was always working on several projects at once and taught me a lot of the crafts that I still use today. Learning just one craft is never enough and even now I still like to learn as much as possible and try my hand at new crafts.

Close-up of the pulled work white rabbit and white ribbonwork roses from Chapter 7.

Large box from my apprenticeship with goldwork, stumpwork and silk shading.

After taking a class in Goldwork Embroidery with Royal School of Needlework graduate Shelley Cox during the school holidays, my passion for embroidery really took off. Little did I know she would later be one of my teachers. It was through Shelley that I found out about the RSN three-year apprenticeship, and was able to progress my skills and become a master of my craft.

I started teaching during my apprenticeship and was given the opportunity to continue teaching day classes while studying for my degree. I had to stop teaching while I concentrated on finishing my degree in Textiles for Fashion and Interiors, specializing in printed textiles, and then worked in Closs and Hamblin fabric shop till I had our son.

For me the joy in box-making is seeing your design become a reality. It is different from stitching an embroidery design because you have to really think about how each box is going to be constructed from start to finish: making one mistake can affect the whole box. While I love every form of embroidery that I studied during my apprenticeship – and each has its own unique challenges – box-making

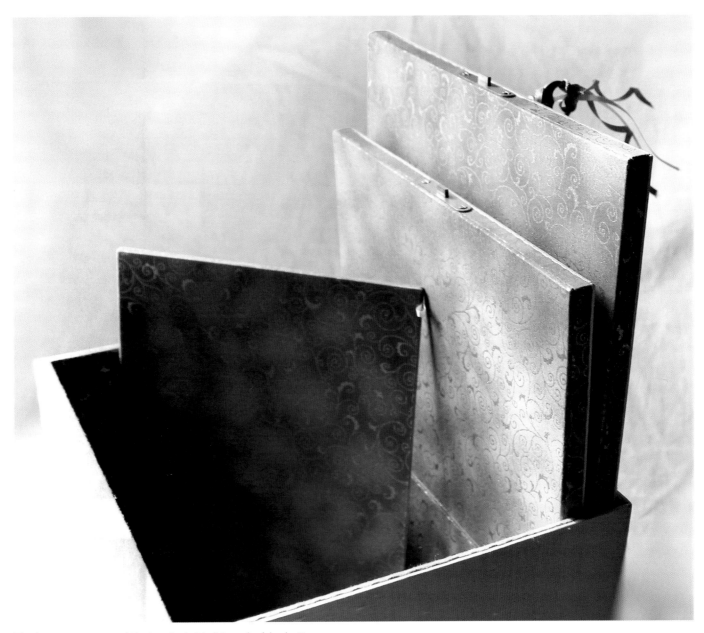

The box opens to reveal the two lockable lids and a false bottom.

was definitely one subject in which I challenged myself further: I wanted to include not one but two working locks within my design, which was based on a box from my favourite fantasy book series by Katharine Kerr.

Once you have mastered the basics of box-making I hope that the instructions in this book will encourage you to design and construct your own boxes. It is vital to complete a detailed design plan, take your time and don't worry if you make a mistake because it can be corrected. You don't have to include embroidery on the boxes if you don't want to but I have tried to include as many different techniques as possible to provide you with inspiration. The more boxes you make the more confident you will become in constructing more challenging designs. My aim is to create modern designs that are adaptable and accessible to everyone, whether you are a beginner or an experienced crafter.

INTRODUCTION

mbroidered boxes were traditionally used to hold a variety of objects, such as jewellery, scent bottles, needlework tools, silver pins and threads, and were often designed for use as writing cabinets. The embroidery on these boxes was originally worked on linen or silk and completed as separate panels for the sides, top and edgings of the lid. The inside panels decorating the drawers were often worked in a flat long stitch with silk floss thread. These panels would usually have a geometric design or stylized flowers and leaves; occasionally they would also have figures and/or animals.

The completed panels would then be sent away to a cabinet-maker who would mount and fit the panels to the chosen box shape. The style of the cabinets varied and many of the later ones were much more elaborate in design than their earlier counterparts, some of which were simply rectangular boxes with a plain lid, like a miniature chest. The later, more complex boxes contained flaps or doors and

some inevitably had 'secret' compartments to hide away treasures. Some had sloping sides, rising steeply like the roof of a house; others had little trays inside, divided up into small compartments to hold tiny objects. The trays would then lift out to leave a large storage space for bigger items. Handles and four ball feet were also attached to some, along with working locks. The trays and drawers were lined with silk, usually in red, pink or blue, which was not used until after 1650. Paper, either patterned or marbled, was used to cover the base and sometimes the inside of the lid if a mirror was mounted inside.

Borders of braid or gimp were stitched onto the outside edges and these varied from a simple neat band to a more complicated lacy trimming of gold thread. The style of figures used on the panels was often similar to those in pictures and complete stories might unfold as different scenes were depicted on each side and on top of the box. The embroiderer would occasionally include in the work a date and initials.

Two famous examples worked by Martha Edlin and Hannah Smith can be found in the Victoria & Albert Museum in London and the Whitworth Art Gallery

in Manchester. The panels embroidered by Martha Edlin for her casket, by the time she was 11 years old, took two years to complete (dated 1671). The top panel is embroidered with the figure of Music playing a lute, while the front and lower sides are representations of the seven virtues: Faith, Hope and Charity, Justice and Temperance, and Fortune and Prudence. They are embroidered on panels of silk satin with tend stitch in silk threads and decorated further with metal threads and purl, silk cord and raised work such as detached buttonhole stitch. The sloping sides at the top are embroidered with a variety of animals including a camel and a unicorn, while the back includes a squirrel between two birds. The casket created by Hannah Smith was made ten years earlier and is in a similar style but the biblical scenes are divided up into scenes of autumn and winter worked in silk, gilt and silver metal on silk satin and canvas. Another beautiful example, worked by soldiers in 1920–30 and now housed at the Museum of New Zealand Te Papa Tongarewa, has blackwork and goldwork embroidered grapes and leaves worked on all of the silk exterior panels.

Boxes made in the late twentieth and early twenty-first century have taken box-making to a new level, although because of progress in technology and manufacturing, it is becoming a rare skill. Boxes are now usually made from fabric-covered card rather than wood, although wood is still used for larger boxes to make them stronger. Some boxes are plain with very little or no embroidery but instead use patterned fabrics, and are very complex in design and structure. Others are very simple boxes with elaborate embroidery on both the interior and exterior. Modern boxes are gradually becoming more and more complicated in terms of shape – they don't have to be restricted to squares and rectangles – however, the more complicated the design the more time-consuming it is to create.

WHY MAKE A BOX?

With the wide availability of manufactured boxes you might be wondering why you should take the time to make your own box. The answer is simply that you can make it to your exact requirements: yours will be more practical than a generic shop-bought box, especially if designed for holding jewellery, because it will be to the size and specification you need as well as personalized and unique to your artistic style. And as well as the challenge of turning an idea on paper into a three-dimensional object, creating something by hand for your keepsakes to be stored in is also a great way to honour them.

There is no better way to show someone your appreciation than to spend time making a box for a special gift. I always appreciate it when someone has made something for me, because I know that they have put a lot of time and effort into creating it.

Stumpwork casket made from panels of silk satin, embroidered with silk and metal threads, mounted onto a wooden casket and signed M.E. for Martha Edlin (1671). ©Victoria and Albert Museum, London.

Close up of the embroidery on a box lid from the author's apprenticeship.

MATERIALS AND EQUIPMENT

aking boxes can require a variety of different materials and equipment; if you are already practising a few different crafts, such as embroidery or card making, then it is likely that you will already have a lot of the necessary equipment. The aim of this chapter is to guide you through all the possible materials and items of equipment that you could need for box-making. It might seem a long list but each box, and the embroidery used to embellish it, varies a great deal. There are only a few set items that will be needed every time you want to make a new box, so the materials and equipment are set out in order of priority with the most important at the beginning. A list of suppliers for most items is available at the back of the book, including those available direct from the author.

Etui box filled with equipment.

Types and thicknesses of conservation card and millboard.

CARD

There are several different types of card that are suitable for box-making, all of which have different benefits depending on the type and style of box you are making. Conservation/museum card, millboard and mount card come in varying thicknesses, measured in micrometres (μm). More commonly called microns, 1000μm is equivalent to 1mm. For box-making, the main card needs to be 1800–2200μm to give a stable base to support both plain and embroidered fabrics. This is not a set rule but I would not want to use a card thinner than 1800μm except in certain circumstances (explained later in the book). Thinner card is likely to bend when the fabric is stretched across it, especially when laced, although this is an advantage when making certain shapes. The card used to create the boxes in this book is 2200μm unless stated otherwise.

Conservation/museum card

Conservation card is acid free, which is likely to make your box last longer than alternatives that are not acid free (if the rest of the materials are also acid free). There are two different types of museum-standard conservation card available: the first has a cotton core, made purely from cotton fibres; the second has a solid core, made from wood fibres that have been chemically purified. Apart from being acid free, the other main advantage of the latter is that is it easy to cut and maintain a smooth, straight edge; it will keep its colour and not turn yellow over time. It is more expensive when compared to other card types, especially the cotton core type, it is not as easy to source as other types of card, and is usually available only in bulk; however, in my opinion the amount of time spent making boxes justifies the cost because you want your masterpiece to last. All of the 2200μm card used in this book is solid core conservation card; because the double-sided tape is not acid free, solid core is perfectly acceptable for the projects in this book. If you were using vintage fabrics or embroidery I would suggest using the cotton core type with acid-free double-sided tape to prolong the life of the fabric.

Millboard

A very dense board made from layers of wood pulp, millboard is often made from recycled or production waste material and is also acid free. Because this board is so densely layered it is slightly harder to cut than other types of board. Millboard is green in colour; it is bleed-proof and light resistant but the downside of this for box-making is that if you are using a thin

fabric (which generally is preferable) the colour of the card can affect the colour of the fabric once it is mounted. This card is significantly cheaper than other types of acid-free board, however, so as long as it will not change the fabric colour drastically it is still worth using, particularly if conservation card is unavailable.

Mount card

This is probably the most readily available type of card, but it is usually available in a standard thickness of 1400μm, is made of wood pulp and tends not to be acid free. This could be used for small boxes in a single layer; two panels can be glued together to create a thicker piece but extra allowances will need to be made for the thickness of the card when cutting the panels. Creating a box with a curve, such as a circle box or chest lid, is best done with this thinner card. If necessary, layers can be carefully removed to make it thinner in order to create the perfect shape.

Hardboard/MDF

Both are made from wood fibres, and are either high- or medium-density fibreboard. MDF is the stronger of the two and doesn't have a rough side like hardboard. These are generally used for very large boxes that need a strong base to keep the box stable, such as a toy box or seat box. Hardboard is generally 3mm thick but MDF is available in varying thicknesses from 3mm to 25mm. If you were to make a toy box or seat a 4–5mm hardboard would be the most suitable as this would be doubled to create the interior and exterior, making the sides between 10 and 12mm thick depending on the fabric used to cover the board.

Needles

Curved needles

A curved needle is the next most important item needed in box-making. There are several different types of curved needle available in a variety of sizes: triangular cutting curved needles, mattress curved needles, and beading and tapestry needles. Triangular cutting needles are available in sizes 10 to 18, with either a 16 or 14 being the recommended sizes to use for box-making. Mattress needles tend to be found in larger sizes (2–7 inches); beading needles are one size and usually long, thin and prone to bending or snapping; tapestry needles are smaller, following the same sizes as their straight counterparts and therefore can be found in a variety of gauges (16–24).

For box-making, a triangular cutting curved needle or a smaller-sized mattress needle can be used because they both have sharp tips which make them effective needles to join the fabric-covered card together. They can pierce the fabric much more easily than a curved tapestry needle, but beware of the sharp tips (I recommend using a thimble with the triangular cutting needles in particular). A curved needle is much easier to sew with than a straight one due to the inflexibility of the card. The smaller-sized needles work particularly well for box-making because the smaller curve of the needle makes stitching the fabric-covered card much quicker. Also, because they are finer they are less likely to damage the fabric than larger needles. Using a curved needle can take a bit of getting used to but once you have the knack you will be stitching quickly in no time. To make the projects in this book a 2-inch mattress needle or a size

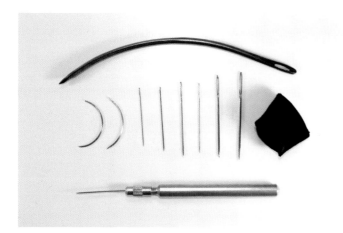

Curved needles, size 10 and 12 sharps, size 26 and 24 tapestry needles, size 9 embroidery/crewel needle, size 20 chenille needle, bracing needle, needle pricker and a handmade leather thimble.

16 triangular cutting needle is needed. Supplier information is available at the back of this book.

NEEDLES FOR EMBROIDERY

There are several different types of needles that are used for embroidery, including sharps, embroidery/crewel, tapestry, chenille and beading. These are all available in a range of sizes; as a general rule of thumb, the higher the number the finer the needle. Several other types of needle are available but these are not relevant for this book. The needle used will depend on the type of embroidery that you are working. Sharps are general embroidery needles and used for most techniques such as silk shading and goldwork; available in sizes 12 to 2, the most common sizes are 10 and 12. Embroidery or crewel needles are used for techniques such as wool crewelwork or stitches that require more than one strand or thicker thread, available in sizes 12 to 1 with the most commonly used being sizes 7 and 9. Tapestry needles are used for several techniques where the threads of the fabric are not pierced but counted and stitched between, such as blackwork, whitework and canvas. Tapestry needles are available in sizes 28 to 13 with the higher numbers being used for finer whitework and blackwork embroideries. Chenille needles have a much larger eye than general sewing needles and a very sharp point which makes them suitable for ribbonwork and crewelwork (the large eye prevents the thread from being damaged as it passes through the fabric). The sharp point makes it easier to stitch through coarse fabrics such as linen and they range in size from 26 to 13 with sizes 20 to 16 being the most commonly used for both techniques.

THIMBLES

It is advisable to use a thimble when using a curved needle, especially with thick and tough fabrics such as leather. I prefer to make my own leather thimbles by cutting out a small rectangle of kid leather, folding in half and over-sewing the edges with a size 12 needle. This allows me to get the perfect fit as I find metal and plastic ones uncomfortable when worn for a few hours and the shop-bought leather thimbles are less flexible.

TAPE AND GLUE

DOUBLE-SIDED TAPE

Available in a variety of widths ranging from 3mm to 25mm and usually not acid free, although there are now some specialist acid-free tapes available. It is only really important to use acid-free tape if you are using a vintage fabric, as this will prolong the life of the fabric. For box-making a 12mm-sized tape is generally the most suitable, as it provides a wider area for the fabric to adhere to and therefore will be more secure than thinner versions. It can also be cut down relatively easily when a thinner strip is required; alternatively the backing tape can be removed and replaced over half of the tape to reduce the thickness on smaller panels of card when a double layer would otherwise be needed to secure both opposite edges of the fabric.

GLUE

There is a vast range of glues available; any clear drying craft or fabric glue that is suitable for both fabric and card is fine. Glue is not used very often during box-making because of the risk of it spreading to unwanted areas. I would therefore use a brand of craft/fabric glue that you are familiar with, as they are all relatively similar. Generally glue is only used to prevent the fabric from fraying when cut or to secure the thread for bead handles to the back of the card panel.

KNIVES AND COMPASS CUTTERS

There are a few different types of knives available for cutting card: retractable utility knives, retractable snap-blade knives and craft knives including mount and compass cutters. Because the card used in box-making is much thicker than standard card a retractable utility knife (such as a Stanley knife) is recommended. The other types of knives are much thinner, prone to snapping and will become blunt more quickly due to the number of scores that are needed to cut through the card. The thickness and weight of a utility knife also make it easier to achieve a smooth and straight edge on the cut edge of the card when applying downward pressure as you cut. The only other type of knife you may need to use is a compass knife, which is used to cut circles out of the card. This has to be done slowly and carefully to achieve a perfect circle, cutting only a few centimetres at a time.

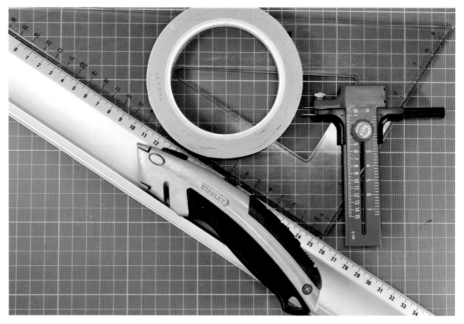
Stanley knife, compass cutter, set square, ruler, double-sided tape and cutting mat.

CUTTING MATS

Self-healing cutting mats are perfect for protecting your work surface when cutting the card; they are available in several sizes ranging from A4 to A2 and are a thick but flexible vinyl and plastic mix. They are usually non-slip, making it easier to apply the correct amount of downward pressure on the card without it slipping. They also have guides printed on them, usually in centimetres, which are useful for checking the card is square after cutting.

METAL RULERS, SET SQUARES AND SHAPE TEMPLATES

Metal rulers are needed not only for measuring the panels of card to be cut but also as a guide to press the knife blade against when cutting. There are three types of metal rulers available: flat, for mount cutting, and safety. Mount-cutting rulers

have two edge types – the first is a fine edge with a ruler for accurate measuring; the other has an upward curve before the cutting edge, to protect fingers, followed by a groove for using a mount cutter as well as an anti-slip rubber strip underneath. Safety metal rulers also have anti-slip strips and are designed with a central recess to protect fingers when cutting. While it is possible to use a flat metal ruler it is best to use either a mount or safety ruler when cutting the thick card because of the anti-slip strips and finger protection.

A set square is another vital piece of equipment in box-making – it is important that each panel is square in order for all the pieces to fit together properly. These can be plastic or metal as they are only used to check that the panel is square before and after cutting rather than as a guide for cutting.

Paper or card templates can be used as a guide for tracing shapes to be cut out, especially those with multiple sides other

Fabric and embroidery scissors. The red-handled pair is used solely for goldwork.

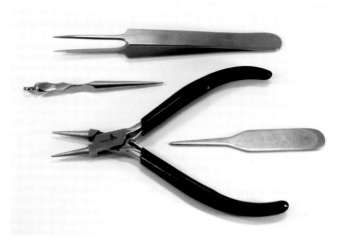

Tweezers, stiletto, pliers and mellor.

than squares. Plastic templates usually used for quilting are also perfect to use instead of paper templates for shaped boxes as they are easy to draw around, can be used more than a couple of times and each shape is available in a variety of sizes.

EMBROIDERY TOOLS

SCISSORS

Ideally you will need fabric, embroidery and paper scissors for box-making; there isn't a set number of scissors that you need and if you are an avid crafter you will probably have several pairs. It can be helpful to have two sizes of fabric scissors available; the larger pair (5 inches or longer) can be used to cut the fabric for each panel and the smaller pair (1½–2 inches) can be used for trimming the fabric when covering the panels. Having more than one type of embroidery scissors is also useful – straight, curved or angled – so that you can always cut the thread as close as possible to the fabric-covered panels.

MELLOR

A mellor, traditionally used in goldwork, is a flat metal tool used to help lay the threads into place without damaging them, but it also has many other uses. It has a flat handle and a tapered rounded point at one end. It is particularly useful in box-making as it can be used to help unpick the stitches when necessary without damaging the fabric. It is used during both lacing and traditional mounting for pulling the stitches tight, as well as for ribbonwork to prevent damaging the fragile silk ribbons.

STILETTO

Traditionally used in the creation of eyelets in whitework, a stiletto can be used for any project in which a circular hole is needed. In box-making it is a useful tool to create holes in the card for attaching handles, either a series of beads threaded onto sewing thread which is then passed through to the back of the card, or for screws from small handles. The stiletto

Hints and tips

It is usually advisable to designate pairs of scissors for particular tasks in order to avoid them becoming blunt too quickly or damaging threads, when cutting goldwork threads or paper, for example. Having a small scissor sharpener as part of your embroidery toolkit is also helpful to maintain the blades. Keeping them as sharp as possible avoids having small tufts of unwanted thread sticking out from the sides of your box.

is made from metal with varying handle designs; it is tapered to a fine but slightly rounded point (much like a tapestry needle) and is used to separate the fabric threads without damaging them.

PLIERS

When sewing with leather or other stiffer fabrics, pliers are essential to save your fingers. Round-nose pliers are preferable as they are gentler on the needle than flat-headed pliers but still provide a good level of grip to help guide the needle through the fabric. If you have only flat pliers available, just be careful that the jagged inside edge doesn't damage the needle as a lot of pressure will be applied to the needle especially when sewing leather.

TWEEZERS

Tweezers are particularly helpful if you have to carefully remove a whole panel from a box or a large section of embroidery and need to remove the cut threads from the fabric without damaging it with the use of scissors. Tweezers with a very long fine point are best, especially when working on smaller boxes, as they will help with hard-to-reach areas and they can also be used to help unpick stitches without damaging the fabric. They are also used when removing tissue paper from fabric during the design transfer process (see Chapter 8 for instructions).

EMBROIDERY FRAMES AND SUPPORTS

Ideally all embroidery (with the exception of smocking) should be worked in some form of frame if the embroidery is going to be mounted onto card, whether it is used for a box or as a piece to be framed. Working embroidery in a frame means that the fabric is worked under the same tension throughout; otherwise the fabric could be distorted by the stitching, caus-

ing ripples or bubbles in the fabric when mounted. The type of frame you use will depend partly on what type of embroidery you are doing – the type of fabric, the size of the design, and how long it is likely to remain in the frame. If you wish to use just one particular type of frame (maybe because it is all you have available or you do not have space to work a larger frame) then it is best to plan and design the embroidery around the size of your frame. There should be an inch or more left between all edges of the design and the edge of the frame, firstly because it is difficult to stitch right up to the edge of the frame and secondly because the frame could damage the threads/materials used if you have to adjust the tension while the embroidery is still being worked.

As all types of embroidery can be worked and mounted for box-making there are lots of different types of frames that you can use. I prefer to use a ring frame with either a seat or table clamp; embroideries for box-making tend to be small and a ring frame is quicker to prepare. It also allows me to work on the sofa or, as I prefer, in a chair with the clamp attached to the desk in my home studio. This enables me to work with both of my hands free and have all of my equipment and materials available on my desk stored safely in my workbox. It may take a bit of practice to get used to working with both hands; I tend to have my dominant hand under the frame and the other above. This makes it easier to be more accurate with my less dominant hand as I can see what I am doing and rely more on instinct with

my dominant hand. Using this technique will help increase the speed at which you stitch as you can pass the needle through the fabric to the hand below and viceversa – much more efficient than working with a single hand.

The fabric can be damaged and creased by leaving it in the frame for too long, and if left uncovered you can also end up with a slight halo where the fabric sandwiched between the two pieces of frame has not been affected by dust and sunlight. There will be some instances where you will not want to remove the fabric from the frame, for instance if you are working whitework with eyelets or drawn thread work, as sometimes removing the fabric (especially if partly completed) can cause more damage or distort the work you have already completed more than keeping it in the frame. Instructions on how to prepare frames for embroidery can be found in Chapter 8 along with the instructions for the embroidery projects.

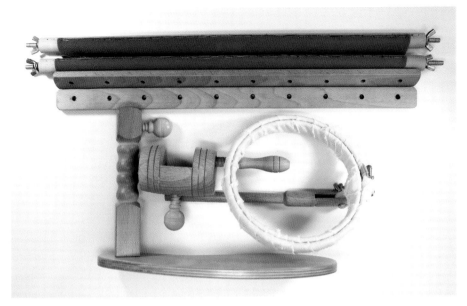

8-inch ring frame, slate frame, table clamp and seat support.

This is a barrel-shaped wooden clamp with a cut-out section in one half. This is slotted over the edge of a desk or table with a wooden screw handle to secure it to the table. There is a hole through the other half of the clamp for the dowel on the ring frame (as described for use with seat frames) with a small plastic screw to hold the dowel in place at the desired height. Depending on the depth of the surface you are attaching it to it is advisable to either use a cutting or protection mat on the top of the table or cover the top inside edge of the clamp with a felt pad, cut to size if needed, to protect the surface. It is always good practice to pack away the frame and clamp once you have finished stitching even if the project isn't completed. If you are working in a dedicated room and will be continuing later or the next day then by all means just remove the fabric but make sure that the embroidery is protected by tissue paper until you are able to continue working on it.

FLOOR STAND

Floor stands come in a variety of different styles, some of which hold the dowel-type ring frames as described above; others have a clamp style fixing to hold either a small slate frame, handheld or dowel-style ring frame. They are either adjustable in height and angle or only height adjustable depending on what type of frame they support. These styles of frame supports are very comfortable to use when adjusted to the correct height and angle as well as having the advantage of being stable enough to be left for a few minutes

HANDHELD RING FRAME

Handheld ring frames are made up of two thin wooden hoops. The smaller one fits inside the larger, which has a break in the circle for a screw tightening mechanism. Handheld frames do have some advantages as they can fit in a tote bag; this is extremely useful if you wish to take your embroidery away from the house. However, the speed at which your embroidery is completed will be slower than with a hands-free frame and if you are using it for a long time your hand may start to cramp from the effort of holding the frame steady as you stitch. Handheld ring frames are available in a wide range of sizes, 4–12 inches, and also have the advantage that they can be used for mounting embroideries.

SEAT FRAME

Ring frames for seat frames are similar to handheld frames but are made up of two thick wooden hoops; the smaller hoop has a hinged dowel attached, which can then be fitted into an upright pillar attached to a shaped base to sit on. The height of the ring frame can be adjusted by moving the dowel up or down within the support pillar, and the angle of the frame can also be adjusted. The base of the seat frame is small enough to fit on most chairs and because the pillar can be removed from the base it is also portable. The pillar can be placed centred or to either side of your legs depending on what is the most comfortable; often once you get used to the frame you won't notice it is there. The ring frames are only available in a small range of sizes (8 inch, 10 inch and 12 inch); however, an adapter clamp with dowel is also available for use with any handheld ring frame in any of the frame supports.

(the seat frames tend to fall over if left unattended). The other advantage is that they can be left set up ready for any spare moments without having to do anything more than set up the fabric or frame again. If you are leaving your work for more than an hour or so it is best to take off the fabric in order to avoid damage, either from the pressure of the frame or from other things falling on it, even with tissue paper covering it. If you are using a slate frame on the stand I would recommend removing it from the clamp and leaning it against something, preferably in a specially made bag (from PVC tablecloth fabric), rather than leaving it attached to the stand in case it gets knocked into another piece of furniture.

SLATE FRAMES

Slate frames are larger wooden frames, usually rectangular. They are available in a variety of sizes (18 and 24 inch are the most popular sizes) and tensioning styles but will always have two roller and two stretcher arms. The two roller arms will have webbing stapled to them for the top and bottom of the fabric to be stitched to. Some types have a hole at each end for the stretcher arms to slot through; others have bolts for the stretcher arms to fit onto or will have peg-like grooves with two positioning holes cut for the stretcher arms. The stretcher arms will either have two sets of holes drilled in a brick pattern on each arm, or they will have a single series of holes for the bolts at each end of the roller arms to be threaded through and tightened with a wing nut. Alternatively they will have a peg-like clip, possibly with two holes to vary the height of the fabric; wing nuts and bolts are then used to keep the roller bars at the correct tension. The latter two styles of frame are slightly less accurate to tension than the first.

All types of slate frame take a long time to set up compared to a ring frame, so are best saved for projects that will take a long time or need to be kept at a set tension. If you will be spending many hours working on a project a slate frame will give you the best final outcome, as the fabric is less distorted by stitches when kept at the correct tension. This is particularly true if you are planning on working more than one design or a very long design that extends beyond the length of the stretcher bars on the same piece of fabric. This can only be done with certain techniques and only where at least one of the embroideries is worked in a flat stitch such as blackwork, which once completed can then be rolled safely around the roller bars without causing damage. By working two designs on the same fabric at the same time you are able to cut out some of the framing-up process; only the webbing on the sides of the fabric will need to be repositioned when the fabric position is changed. The other advantage of a slate frame over a ring frame is that if you are working a large design you might not be able to reach the middle of your work comfortably, in which case it is useful to be able to roll the fabric around the arms so that a smaller central section of the design can be reached and then rolled out each side until the whole of the design has been worked. I would never recommend moving a ring frame around the fabric to complete a larger design, as the sides of a ring frame will crease, distort and squash any stitches that have already been worked. Instructions for setting up a slate frame can be found in Chapter 8 with the embroidery projects.

PENS, PENCILS AND PAINTS

PENS

Pens can be used to transfer designs onto fabric; they must be permanent, especially if you are likely to need to wash the fabric before mounting onto a box panel or in a frame. It is always a good idea to test the pen on a small piece of the fabric you will be using, both to check that it is indeed permanent (some can still run) and to check that the line drawn does not spread more than expected and distort the design to be worked. Using a pen with a very fine tip will help with this but even these can spread, especially if you press slightly harder than intended against the fabric.

There are permanent fabric pens available specifically for use on textiles; if you are used to crafting with fabrics then you will probably have used pens which are either water soluble, disappear over time or can be ironed away. These are not ideal for this purpose, as the drawing can either last longer than expected or disappear before you are finished, if it is a particularly large design. The use of iron-away pens very much depends on what type of embroidery you are working on – the last thing you want to do is flatten or damage the stitches when ironing close to the embroidery. With water-soluble pens you will need to test your threads and fabric to ensure that they are colourfast; while most modern threads are colourfast this is not always guaranteed with older threads.

Fabric pencils, paintbrush and permanent pen.

Light pad, clamp and handheld magnifying glass.

Hints and tips

PENCILS

For marking the cutting lines I would use an HB propelling pencil: they don't have to be sharpened to maintain a fine point and the line won't distort as you draw. The cutting lines need to be as thin and accurate as possible. Either a 0.8mm or 0.5mm pencil lead will give you the most accurate cutting line.

To mark a design on fabric there are permanent pencils available. For white-work I would definitely use a light blue permanent pencil rather than a pen, as it is less likely to show between or through the stitches. It is also possible to buy a propelling pencil with leads specifically designed for use on fabric. The ceramic leads are available in white, yellow, green, black and pink; they can be changed and used exactly the same as a standard lead propelling pencil. Like other propelling pencils they also come with a rubber to use should you make a mistake. Personally I prefer to use pencils rather than pens (except on canvas) because a lighter line is produced which is more forgiving than pen. You may find that the pencil lines will fade slightly as you work but as it is a pencil it is possible to go over the lines again while stitching without risking the colour bleeding onto the stitches already worked or having to wait for it to dry completely.

PAINT

For very dark fabrics or designs that will take a long time to embroider, paint is the best medium to use for transferring the design. Because darker fabrics are harder to see through when using a lightbox, a more accurate method is the prick and pounce method with ground-up cuttlefish (instructions in Chapter 8) followed by painting with gouache. Using a very fine brush (size 0000), a thin line of gouache is painted straight onto the fabric. Do not use any water, as this would cause the paint to bleed. Once dry any thicker parts of the paint can be carefully picked off with a needle as you stitch.

LIGHTBOXES, LIGHTING AND MAGNIFICATION

LIGHTBOX

Lightboxes were originally boxes with a piece of glass or plastic on the top with a light placed behind to enable designs to be copied either onto paper or fabric. Most lightboxes available for purchase nowadays tend to be ultra-slim: two flat pieces of plastic glued together, like a computer tablet. This makes them more portable and saves space as they can be tucked away in a drawer when not in use and are available to fit A4 and A3 paper. While it is unlikely that a beginner in box-making would be working larger than A4, it is entirely possible to create larger boxes. I have found the A4 lightbox size to be quite generous and unless you are working right to the edges on an A3 piece of paper it would easily be big enough to work with larger designs. Instructions for design transfer can be found in Chapter 8.

Buttonhole and machine threads.

MAGNIFICATION

For very fine embroidery techniques, such as blackwork or whitework, you may need a magnifying glass to help with the accuracy of counting threads or for viewing intricate stitches more closely. As well as small, handheld versions, magnifying glasses for embroidery are available with a clamp attached to secure to the frame; they also come attached to daylight lamps. It can take some practice to get used to using a magnifying glass and some people prefer not to use them while they are stitching but just occasionally for checking work. In this case a handheld glass can be more useful as it is less likely to get in the way. Do not place the glass too close, either to the fabric or your eyes, and take regular breaks to rest your eyes by looking at objects further away. Getting up to make a drink is a good way to have a break away from your work and will allow you to relax for a good amount of time before continuing. If you find that you are having difficulty seeing stitches when working close to the fabric – with or without a magnifying glass – it is worth booking an eye test, to check that there isn't an underlying issue that you might not otherwise be aware of.

While you will want to ensure that you have the best light possible when using a magnifying glass, working close to a window perhaps, it is important to make sure that the magnifying glass is not placed in direct sunlight (whether or not it is in use), as a magnifying glass in direct sunlight could cause the fabric to catch fire.

DAYLIGHT LAMPS

When stitching an embroidery or joining together box panels, it is very important to have good lighting in the room you are working in, in order to protect your eyes and to see what you are working on in fine detail. Daylight lamps are very useful and come in a variety of styles – small table lamps, tall floor lamps, clip-on, clamp style – and are also available as single bulbs that can be fitted into existing lamps and ceiling lights. Artificial lights can sometimes affect how our eyes see the colour of threads and fabrics, because they emit yellow rather than white light, so it is important for the overall finish of the embroidery to make sure that the correct lighting is in place, as it may look very different in daylight if only artificial lighting is used. Using daylight bulbs also ensures that no matter what time of day you stitch in most, you will always have the same level of light to work in.

The style of lamp that you choose will depend on where you spend the majority of your time stitching or crafting, but I would recommend researching them first to see what will best fit your needs. Ideally for box-making you will need a work desk in order to cut out the panels of card and to support the panels as you join them together. I have three different lamps on my desk because it gives me the best lighting possible, even on a dull day. Two of them are smaller desk lamps with clamp adapters and a flexi-tube for maximum adjustment; the other can either be a floor lamp or clamped to a desk with various (but slightly more limited) levels of adjustment. I also have daylight bulbs in my ceiling light to make my work more accurate and because I find that any artificial light will affect the colour of what I am working on. There used to be only one type of daylight bulb available, which was relatively expensive, but there is now a much wider range of bulbs available in many shops, and at a more reasonable price; just ensure that 'daylight' rather than just 'white light' is specified on the box.

Threads and Embroidery Materials

Machine sewing threads and buttonhole thread

The box panels are stitched together using a mixture of machine sewing threads and buttonhole thread, also known as top-stitch thread. These threads are mainly made from polyester because it is a stronger and longer-lasting thread than cotton (although cotton machine threads are available I would only use it if you cannot find a close enough colour in polyester). Various machine sewing thread brands are available on the high street and come in a vast array of colours, although craft stores are likely to stock a selection from the entire range. Buttonhole thread is usually available in a slightly more limited colour range and is a heavyweight thread, thicker than general machine sewing thread. While it is slightly elastic it is tear- and abrasion-resistant which makes it perfect for lacing, mounting and for box hinges or cupboard doors that have a lot of weight or use. It therefore shouldn't break when placed under the tension needed for lacing and mounting, or snap from overuse or the weight from a lid or cupboard door that has a lock mounted within it.

It is important to try and choose a colour of machine sewing thread as close to that of the fabric you will be working with as possible – although your stitches should not be visible when using ladder stitch. Buttonhole thread to be used for lacing can be any colour but I generally tend to use a white or cream colour. When a perfect match of machine sewing thread is not available it is a matter of personal judgement; it is usually better to go with

Stranded cottons stored by brand and colour type.

a thread that is slightly lighter in colour rather than darker. If the fabric has multiple colours it is best to choose a thread that is sympathetic to all of the colours in the fabric. For instance, if the fabric were a mix of yellow, light and dark green (like the drawer in Chapter 4) then I would go with a thread to match the light green as it should not be too noticeable on the yellow or dark green. If you have trouble choosing between several options then a little trick is to place the number of strands you will be using, usually only one or two, on the fabric you will be using. Hold them roughly at half arm's length and squint your eyes slightly; whichever is the least visible is the one you should go with.

Stranded cottons

Made from 100 per cent cotton, stranded cottons are probably the most used thread for embroidery because they are so versatile; they come in hundreds of different shades and are easy to work with. There are several different brands available, each with a slightly different range but they are always produced in a 6-ply or 6-strand skein (6 separate strands twisted together), usually 8m in length. There are no rules dictating how many strands you can use in the needle at a time, but it is important to use the correct-sized needle for the number of strands you wish to use in order to avoid causing wear on the thread. It is generally advisable to separate the strands and then group them back together prior to use, in order for them to lie flat and not have loops where individual strands have shifted as you work. (There may be an odd occasion where this rule needs to be broken in order to maintain the twist on the thread rather than using individual strands.) I find 'stranding' is easiest to do when holding the six strands securely between thumb and forefinger of your less dominant hand; use your dominant hand to pull the strands one at a time from the group. This should be done using only the short length of thread you will be stitching with, usually 20–30cm. This way they will not become tangled and you can also just separate the number of strands you need for the thickness of stitch you require while keeping the rest together. I also prefer to wind the cotton around card bobbins to avoid tangles and for ease of storage, with different brands stored in separate boxes.

PERLÉ AND COTON FLOCHE

Also made from 100 per cent cotton, perlé is a silky single strand 2-ply twisted thread, used straight from the skein. Perlé is available in a variety of different thicknesses and colours and is a lovely thread to work with. Care must be taken not to use too long a length (no longer than 30cm) because the thread can start to untwist as you work. Replace as soon as it starts to look worn, especially if working with more than one length on canvas; this is because the density of the stitches will make the thread wear more quickly than if worked individually though a different fabric.

Coton floche is a 5-ply mercerized cotton thread, worked straight from the skein. It is usually used in whitework designs or embroidery when a thicker single thread is required. It can be used as a surface thread or as padding underneath satin stitches or thicker sections of trailing. Because it usually comes in a 10g skein it is advisable to plait the skein and cut the loops at one end so that the threads are a workable length when pulled out; this will make them easier to remove and avoid tangles.

WOOL

There are various sizes of wool, all of which come in a wide variety of colours. Crewel wool is the most used type for fine embroidery, and the 2-ply thread is also used straight from the skein. Due to its delicate nature care needs to be taken to check for wear on the thread, as the more it is passed through the fabric the weaker it will become. Again it is important to keep the lengths short and replace as soon as any damage or thinning is visible. Wools have fallen out of fashion in recent years and so therefore may not be readily available in high-street craft shops but there are several brands available for purchase online.

GOLDWORK THREADS

Gold or metal embroidery threads are available in such a wide range of styles and colours now that there are too many to list them all. Traditional forms of the threads, and arguably the best quality, are produced solely in the UK by a few small companies. It is even possible to buy threads made of real gold but these are very expensive and can tarnish more quickly than gilt threads. Due to the nature of the materials and the processes used to make them, metal threads are relatively expensive and therefore it is important to plan your embroidery carefully to make sure that you can purchase enough of the types you need. The threads are very delicate and can be easily damaged so it is important to store them properly. They should be sold in acid-free bags so it is important that they remain in these. This is another way of telling the quality of the thread; those sold in plastic packets or boxes, while still perfectly usable, are usually of lower quality.

The threads can be divided into three types. The first and second are pure metal threads, either hollow (pearl purl, check and purl) or flat (spangles and plate). Depending on the type, the securing thread is either invisibly couched between the twists or the needle is passed through the hole like a bead and stitched into place. The third type of thread consists of metallic paper wrapped around a cotton core (Japanese, rococo, passing, check or twist); this is couched into place either singly or in pairs with a sympathetic colour of sewing thread or a contrasting one. Goldwork is different from other types of embroidery in that the threads are laid on top of the fabric and secured with a separate waxed sewing thread that ideally you do not want to see. With couching techniques it is not possible for the thread to be hidden as it is passed over the gold threads to secure them; to make them less noticeable, choose a thread colour as close as possible to the colour of the metal. There is a form of goldwork called *or nué* which uses different coloured threads, sometimes silk, to create an image or shading within the gold threads. The couched threads then need to be finished off neatly by 'plunging' them through the fabric one at a time and then securing to the back by oversewing a small length (roughly 1cm) of the thread with a waxed piece of the sewing thread.

Goldwork is probably one of my favourite techniques to work; the range of thread types and techniques is so vast that the embroidery possibilities are almost endless. Some techniques are more difficult to master than others, however, and because the threads are unlike any others they are less forgiving. It is therefore advisable to practise with them before working on the final design. Always use a separate pair of scissors kept specifically for cutting metal threads for goldwork because they can cause damage and make them blunt. It is also important to make sure that the sewing thread used is adequately waxed by drawing it through a piece of pure beeswax several times (so that it squeaks when pulled between your fingers) to help prevent the metal from snagging and damaging the threads. As with other types of embroidery it is very important to keep the sewing thread length short and replace as soon as it looks worn; it is far easier to replace a slightly worn thread than a snapped thread that could risk damaging the work you have already completed. For more information about goldwork materials please see the Further Reading section at the back of this book.

RIBBONS

Ribbonwork is a technique which is very much coming back into fashion, and for the best results is it definitely worth using only pure silk threads or possibly organza as these threads are very delicate and more open to manipulation than thicker satin and grosgrain ribbon. It is well worth the

Goldwork thread materials, including blue rough, gilt bright check, leathers, beeswax, yellow string, velvet board, rococo, gold and silver spangles.

effort to find pure silk ribbons; they can be relatively expensive compared to the other types of ribbon, especially those that are hand dyed, but you usually won't need more than a few metres of each colour in a small project – it is surprising how little some techniques need. They are usually available to purchase by the metre or in small packs; it is always worth ordering more than you think to be sure that you have enough as the shades are more likely to vary compared to other types of threads. They are available in a variety of widths (2–13mm) and colours, including variegated types. They are also available in white or undyed, both of which are suitable for you to dye should you wish. Hand dyeing often produces irregular results that are difficult to replicate especially if they are variegated. It is therefore worth dyeing much more than you think you will need to ensure you have enough to finish your project; any ribbon left can always be used for future projects. For more information about ribbonwork materials please see the Further

Reading section at the back of this book.

Ribbon supports for box hinges, tags on lids and to secure items in place on sides can be made using any type of ribbon: satin, grosgrain ribbon or ric-rac will provide the best level of support as they are far stronger and less delicate than silk or organza ribbons. The width of ribbon that you choose will depend on the size of the box you are making; most likely you will only need a smaller size, 4–13mm.

BEADS AND CRYSTALS

Beads and crystals are available in such a wide range of colours, sizes and shapes that I would need another book to discuss them all. The important thing to bear in mind when choosing beads and crystals for your box, whether they are to be included within the embroidery or as a handle for a drawer or cupboard, is that they are good-quality glass beads or Swarovski crystals.

HANDLES, MIRRORS AND LOCKS

Any small screw can be used for box handles, or you can make your own. It's important to try and choose the size of the handle so that it works for the size of the box you are making; you don't want it to be too big or too small. Larger glass beads can be combined with smaller beads to create handles, or it is possible to use polymer clay which has been moulded around a nut and bolt and baked in the oven till hard (following the guidelines on the packet). The nut is kept within the clay while it bakes but the screw can be removed prior to this. Plumbing compression olives can be used to obtain a perfectly round shape and then the clay can be removed from them after baking.

Mirrors should ideally be made of a thin glass and not too big and heavy for the size of the box, with enough room left to secure the edges to the back of the recess cut in the card for it. There are two types of lock suitable for box making: mortice (or cupboard locks) and box locks (for fitted hinged lids). Which type you use will depend on the position required for your box to lock. Whichever you choose the size also needs to be appropriate for the size of the box.

FABRICS

A wide range of fabrics can be used for box-making, and there are no set rules as to which type of fabric can be used for certain boxes, although it's important to bear in mind that some fabrics will have limited uses, such as leather. There are a

Polymer clay handles with compression olive moulds.

few aspects to consider when deciding on the fabric to be used for your box:

- A thinner fabric is better than a thicker one, as there will be less bulk on the back of the covered panels.
- The type of embroidery you will be working will also dictate which fabric is most suitable; if a thinner and more delicate fabric like silk is used then you will need to consider a backing of lightweight calico for the embroidered section to support the weight of the embroidery.
- The weave of the fabric is also important: if the fabric is very loosely woven then there is a risk that the card will be visible through the fabric once mounted. In this case it is best to use loosely woven or sheer fabrics only on the exterior of the box so that a more tightly woven fabric can be mounted onto the card first – either in a matching colour or contrasting – followed by the chosen fabric.
- Avoid using fabrics with too much

stretch, such as jersey, as the fabric is only secured onto the back of the card. The risks are that the fabric will move around on the card more than desired, affecting the fit and stability of the box, or that a lot of tension would need to be applied to prevent this, and the card might show through.
- If using a patterned fabric you will need to consider whether the pattern should match up from panel to panel or if it can just have a random placement as long as the direction of the pattern remains the same. Similarly, if using a 'shot' fabric (where two or more colours are combined in the warp and weft, so the colour appears to change from different directions) it is important to maintain the correct direction on all pieces of fabric.
- If using leather, consider whether it is suitable for the whole exterior of the box or only certain parts. Because of the way it is secured to the card it is not suitable for use on very small panels.

Clockwise from top left: felt, even-weave linen, calico, coloured sateen backing fabric, bump and cotton fabric from the drawer in Chapter 4.

Hints and tips

- If you are mounting a linen or other loose-weave fabric to a panel then I would recommend using a plain-coloured quilting cotton rather than calico over the card first. Particularly when whitework techniques have been used, such as eyelets or drawn threads, the use of a coloured background during mounting can help to enhance the embroidery, as it will be visible beneath the white of the linen.
- Keep a record in a 'dye book' of the quantities and colours used alongside a scrap of the dyed fabric. This will make it much easier to replicate colours. If possible, purchase a set of scales that can weigh amounts smaller than a gram (this can also be useful when using goldwork techniques, to keep track of the amounts you have used).

Natural fabrics such as cotton, silk, linen, leather and wool are, in my opinion, the best fabrics to work with because they usually feel and look far superior to synthetic materials, although there are also some very lovely natural and synthetic mixes available.

Synthetic fabrics can be used in some circumstances: I have used a synthetic crushed shimmer fabric for the pentagon-shaped box, which works very well with the goldwork on the box. With the advancement of technology some synthetic fabrics can feel and look very much like natural ones; for example, acrylic, a type of plastic fabric made from acrylic acid which feels very much like cashmere, is a useful soft fabric to use if you have allergies to natural fabrics.

FABRICS FOR BACKING AND PADDING

Calico is used to back fabrics that need extra support when being embroidered and to cover the card. It is 100 per cent cotton and available in a variety of different weights but I would recommend using a lightweight calico to avoid adding unnecessary bulk to the back of the panels. Felt, bump (cotton curtain interlining) and fusible interlining are all used as padding, either for the internal panels or the exterior lid tops as padding behind the embroidery to ensure it looks even after lacing or mounting. Fusible interlining is used when more support is needed than felt or bump can provide; it can even replace the use of card in boxes where you may wish to store pins or needles on the interior panels, such as the etui box in Chapter 5.

FABRIC AND THREAD DYES

Machine and cold hand dyes are readily available and also easy to use for dyeing fabrics and threads. Procion specialist dyes can also be found in specialist art and craft shops or online; these allow much more flexibility of colour because they can be mixed more easily than other dye types; the colours are stored separately from the fixatives making it easier to mix and test colours before using them. Fabrics can also be dyed using natural dyes such as tea or beetroot – but this will require a lot of experimentation.

CHAPTER 2

BASIC CONCEPTS OF CONSTRUCTION

ethods of box construction have evolved considerably over the years, and it is my preference to make use of technological advances while still maintaining the essence of a traditional craft. In this chapter I will be using both modern and traditional techniques to construct the boxes, using conservation card as the main support system for the fabric. I have included several methods to secure the fabric to the card: double-sided tape for the unembroidered sides, and traditional lacing and mounting techniques for securing the embroidered lids or sides. This is because it is important that the embroidery is mounted securely to the card to ensure there are no wrinkles and the design stays in the correct position. The basic stages of construction, such as cutting the card, taping or lacing, and stitching panels together, do not vary by much from box to box; it is the additional steps (different shapes and added decora-

tive and functional elements) that make some boxes more complex. Once you have mastered the basics in this chapter you will then be able to branch out to more complex designs.

All of the boxes in this book can be adapted to fit your own requirements but I would recommend starting with the small gift box at the end of this chapter. You can increase the size if you wish but I would avoid adding any additional elements until you have gained confidence from creating a smaller version. This is a simple box with few processes – similar to the one I created during my apprenticeship, which was an invaluable experience in helping me to understand the basic principles.

It is important that during the construction process you keep your workspace as free of clutter as possible, while still having access to all of the equipment you might need. Having enough space on your desk or table means that you are less likely to cause accidental damage to the box or

materials you are using. This is especially important if you are cutting from a large piece of card; the card needs to be completely flat when cutting so try to ensure the desk does not require a tidy-up every time you wish to cut out a panel. If space is limited, a small three-tier trolley can be useful to store equipment when it's not being used; this can be tucked under the desk ready for use at all times.

Use a comfortable chair at the correct height so that your feet are planted flat on the floor, and take regular breaks. With box-making you will need to be standing to cut the card in order to apply the correct amount of pressure; this is a good opportunity to have a little stretch and look around the room to allow your eyes to adjust after the close-up work you have been doing.

Ideally non-embroidered fabric should be ironed and rolled onto a cardboard tube to prevent creases while being stored.

Small gift box with
heart embroidery.

MEASURING AND CUTTING THE CARD

Using a metal ruler and a set square, measure the first panels of card. I prefer to use a propelling pencil to mark the lines because it makes a finer line than a normal pencil line, reducing the chances of the measurements varying. If starting with a new piece of card you can generally use the fresh sides as they are but it is still important to make sure that they are definitely square before you start; this will make things easier when joining the pieces together. I prefer to use a ruler specifically designed as a mount cutter because it is slightly shaped for a better grip and also has a rubber strip along one of the bottom edges to prevent it from slipping (this can happen with a flat ruler no matter how much pressure is applied).

Measure and cut each set or group of sides as you go, because the knife may change the measurements slightly as it cuts and you can then make any necessary adjustments. In order to keep the sizes consistent where the panels have a side of the same length I suggest that you measure a long length and then cut the other panels from the long piece. For instance, if the four interior sides are all 4.4cm high, mark this measurement in several places, parallel to the edge of the card, then draw the line in one continuous length to cover all of the sides with a bit of excess and cut one by one. Then divide the strip into the other sizes needed for the front, back and sides, which should differ in their pairs. It is important to start with the interior pieces first; this is because the thickness of the material and card you are using could change the measurements of the outside pieces. Generally if you are using

The best way to hold the knife when cutting is at a slight angle with the blade pressed against the metal ruler.

thin quilting cotton or a silk the change in the measurements should be minimal. The use of linen or leather fabric could potentially change the measurements by a millimetre or more, however, so this will need to be taken into account when cutting the card. Only cut the exterior sides once the interior has been constructed; it is always best to work from the interior out unless directed otherwise within the chapters.

A retractable Stanley knife is usually the best tool for cutting the card because it is sharp and heavy-duty enough to cut through thick card. A Stanley knife is also fine enough not to drastically change the measurements – if you find that it does you can always adjust the measurements by a millimetre or so as necessary and recut the affected pieces. It is possible to use a 90° mount cutter but I find that you have to be very precise when aligning the blade to make sure that you cut along the correct line.

When cutting it is important to start by just lightly scoring the card with a small amount of pressure; then increase the pressure on the second and following cuts. The thickness of the card means that it is important to cut with more than one or two strokes because this will allow for greater accuracy. The first score will act as a guide to prevent the knife going off course. Having a nice crisp, clean edge on the card is paramount to ensure that your box will have clean, even edges. If there are small nicks in the edges of the card then it can be sanded lightly with a fine sandpaper but this should be done with extreme care in case it should change the measurements. The knife should be held so that your knuckles are touching the card and therefore the length of the blade is used rather than just the tip.

To cut out a circle using a compass circle cutter, carefully and lightly score the entire circumference of the circle, then pressing harder cut through the card in small sections (3–4cm) before moving on to the next section. This is a slow process but your circles will be a better shape and more accurate if extra time is taken to cut them out.

FABRIC PLACEMENT

A stripy box from the author's collection with an appliqué Scottie dog in plaid, outlined with a couched metallic thread. This shows how stripes can be placed so that the continuity of the pattern flows across the box.

It is very important when planning a box to think about how you want the fabric to look when it is laced or taped to the card. As a general rule of thumb, have the grain of the fabric running from top to bottom, although in some cases where the colour of the fabric changes, such as a silk with different warp and weft colours, you may want to position the fabric to take advantage of one colour more than the other. Or there might be a pattern on the fabric that you want to work in a certain way with the design of the embroidery. Whatever you decide, as long as you are cutting all the pieces in the same direction and not using the bias grain it shouldn't create any problems with the overall construction of the box. There may be a few occasions when the bias is used, to achieve a certain shape or when a little more stretch is needed from the fabric.

I would avoid using stripes unless they precisely follow the grain of the fabric, or are on a very obvious diagonal, as it will be apparent when they are stretched over the card if they are not straight. If you do decide to use stripes or another small repeat pattern you will need to think carefully about the pattern placement on each panel of the box it is used to cover. For instance if you use a stripe, you may want to make sure that the stripe direction is continued and lined up from the base of the box to the lid (as in the photograph). The amount of fabric you have available will also dictate whether you are able to pattern match across the panels (*see* the Etui box in Chapter 5). With only a small amount of fabric available and a large repeat, I decided not to match the pattern across the large panels. With the striped box I was able to match the pattern because the repeat was small and there was plenty of fabric to be able to choose exactly where the pattern would sit on each panel so that the stripes flow from the box sides up to the lid.

DOUBLE-SIDED TAPE AND GLUE

While lacing or mounting is the appropriate method for the embroidered elements, double-sided tape speeds up the process of covering the plain sides of the box and is a very good method of securing the fabric while it is being stitched into place. The tape should be very easy to tear so it can be placed along the side of the card and torn, rather than cut with scissors.

I would not advise using glue to secure the fabric to the card, except to prevent fraying or during traditional mounting, because it can spread to areas of the fabric where it isn't wanted, making stitching the pieces together more difficult. And in the time it takes to dry you could have laced or taped the fabric to the card, so it doesn't save time. If glue is just being used to prevent fraying on the edges I would suggest instead that you use an overlocker or wide zigzag stitch on the sewing machine, which would be more efficient and less risky than using glue. Leave a larger seam allowance where possible so the stitched edges can be trimmed away to avoid adding extra bulk once the fabric is secured to the card.

GENERAL CONSTRUCTION TECHNIQUES

The following pages provide you with step-by-step methods for covering the card, mitring, lacing and ladder stitch – these are the same throughout this book unless specific instructions say otherwise. The process and construction order for each type of box, lid, drawer or cupboard changes for each box depending on the style being constructed.

COVERING THE CARD WITH FELT

While lids are regularly covered with felt padding, you may on occasion also wish to cover the card for the interior panels with felt to add padding to protect the items you are storing in the box. For an exterior lid panel the felt can cover the entire panel of card prior to being mounted with the embroidered fabric; the felt can either be attached to the card with double-sided tape or left loose. If possible, use a pre-cut corner of the felt so that you only have to cut two sides; the edges of the card can be used as a guide to cut along, ensuring that the felt is cut as straight as possible without any jagged edges.

If you are covering the internal sides of a box or dividers then you will need to cut the felt smaller than the card it is being attached to in order to leave a space for any other panels that will connect to it. For instance the base will have a gap, the thickness of the card, on all sides for the sides of the box to sit in. Dividers that have padding will also need to have gaps left for any connecting dividers to fit into, to avoid adding extra length to the connecting

1. Stick double-sided tape to the back of the card to be covered with felt.

2. Stick the card in the corner of the felt and cut the other two sides as straight as possible.

3. Trim the edges of the felt with fabric scissors to give a neat, rounded edge.

divider. In these instances it is best to secure the felt with double-sided tape so that it stays in the correct place once the panel is covered with the desired fabric.

COVERING THE CARD USING DOUBLE-SIDED TAPE

You will need

- Fabric
- Panel of conservation card
- Double-sided tape
- Small fabric or straight embroidery scissors

1. Iron and cut the fabric for the panel so that it is approximately 1.5–2cm bigger on each edge than the card and the grain is running parallel with the edges of the card. Placing the panel top to bottom, stick a piece of double-sided tape along the top and bottom edges leaving a small gap before the edge of the card.

2. Peel off the tape paper and fold the top section down first onto the tape and then the bottom, pulling up slightly so the fabric is taut against the card and the grain follows the edges of the card.

3. The fabric then needs to be trimmed back to the edge of the tape and at a diagonal across the corners, leaving approximately 5mm of fabric before the corner of the card to reduce the bulk created when folded.

4. Attach more tape to the side edges, again leaving a small gap between the tape and the edges of the card.

5. Peel off the tape paper on one side and then, tucking in the overlapping piece of fabric in the corners with your fingernails, fold over the fabric to leave a straight, neat edge.

6. Do the same on the remaining side, making sure the fabric is taut and following the grain of the fabric; trim any excess fabric from the back.

Starting and finishing threads using a holding stitch

Threads for embroidery should always be started and finished where possible using a holding stitch within the design area. This method avoids knots creating a bumpy surface and gives a better finish once the embroidery is mounted or laced. Starting a thread for embroidery with the knot on top, stitch down into an area of the design to be embroidered, and make two or three small stitches, preferably less than a millimetre in size, to secure the thread, then cut the knot off. This same method is used to finish a thread, as long as the stitches are not going to be visible. However, it is not always possible to avoid the stitches showing, such as for blackwork or canvas work. If this is the case, starting with the knot on top as before, stitch down either in the area to be embroidered or outside the design area. Work the thread in the desired stitch and only when the thread is secured (test by pulling the knot and watching for any movement in the stitches) can the knot be removed from the surface. The thread is sometimes secured by itself as you work over the area of the design or it may need to be secured once the embroidery is complete by weaving it between the reverse stitches on the back of your embroidery using a lasso in the needle for shorter lengths.

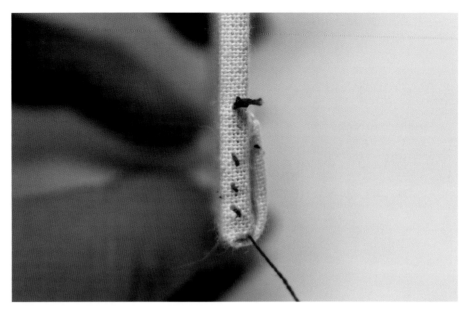

Close-up of a holding stitch on a box panel prior to the knot being removed.

Starting a thread to sew box sides together is similar to the method used when starting embroidery designs but instead of starting the thread in a design area, start on the reverse side of the card where the fabric has been taped or laced or on the edge of a panel that will be hidden. The thread is finished in the same way with small stitches and again on the reverse side of the card or edge. There will be times when it is not always possible to start or finish using the small stitches because there are no reverse/hidden areas available. When this is the case it is best to secure the thread by working a ladder holding stitch.

You will need

- Pre-covered panels of card
- Sewing thread of a matching colour
- Small fabric or straight embroidery scissors

Ladder stitch, also sometimes known as slip stitch, is the method used to stitch together two separate edges as seamlessly as possible. This is the main stitch used in box-making, and with a small amount of practice, even if you have not used a curved needle before, this is a very simple stitch to master. On most occasions you will be able to start and finish the ladder stitch using a standard holding stitch by hiding the stitches on the wrong side of one of the panels you are joining. When this is not possible, a ladder holding stitch will enable you to start and finish the thread invisibly without having to hide the stitches (*see* next page). I have used a contrasting thread in order for you to see the stitches clearly; usually you would choose a thread to match the colour of the fabric.

1. Secure the sewing thread to one of the panels (A) to be joined in a place where it will not be seen using a fine curved needle.

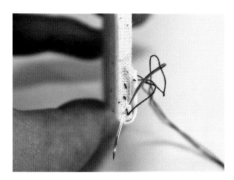

2. Carry the needle under the fabric to the corner of the panel to be joined and pull the thread all the way through.

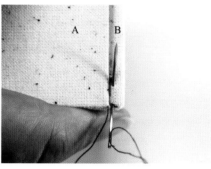

3. Holding both panels next to each other, pierce the fabric on the opposite panel (B) at the adjacent point to the end of the thread. Carry the needle under the fabric for approximately 3–4mm and then bring it back through the fabric.

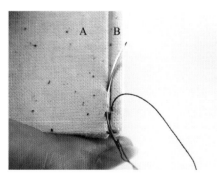

4. Cross back over to panel (A), piercing the fabric adjacent to the end of the previous stitch, and carry the needle under for 3–4mm before bringing to the surface again.

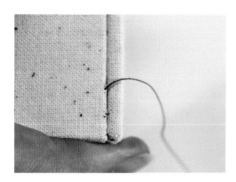

5. The thread can then be pulled gently until the two panels are brought together and the thread is hidden to create an invisible join.

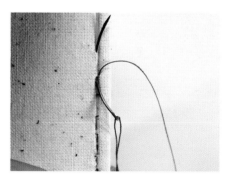

6. Continue stitching the panels together, making sure to keep the stitch spacing as even as possible, until they are completely joined and the thread can be securely finished in an area which will not be visible.

LADDER HOLDING STITCH

Ladder holding stitch is usually used in the final stages of construction and for hinges when there are no wrong sides of panels or other areas to hide the starting and finishing stitches. Both the starting and finishing holding stitches are worked in the same way but the finishing stitches need to be started when there is a gap of about 6–7 standard size stitches left before the end of the panels you are joining; triple stitch length spaces can be left rather than double if you want to make the finishing stitches extra secure. The idea of the ladder holding stitch is to create an invisible anchor to secure the thread by working extra long stitches and then weaving back along the stitches to fill in gaps between them.

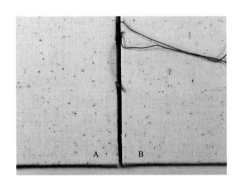

1. With a knot on the end of the thread carry the needle under the fabric a double stitch length on the panel you are joining (A).

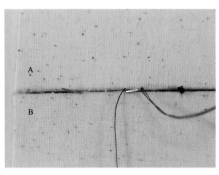

2. Crossing over to the other panel (B), pierce the fabric adjacent to the thread and carry the needle under for another double stitch length before bringing to the surface.

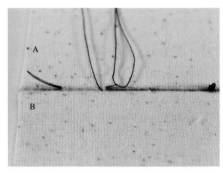

3. Cross back over to the first panel (A) and again stitch under the fabric another double length stitch.

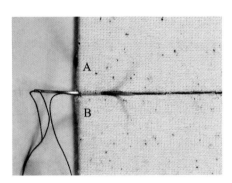

4. Take a final stitch into the corner and then turn the needle back in the direction you have just worked, and stitch under a normal stitch length on the second panel.

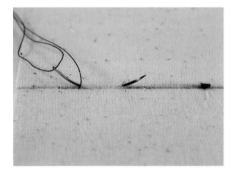

5. Continue working back between your previous stitches, filling in the gap between the first stitches so that they are spaced roughly 3–4mm apart.

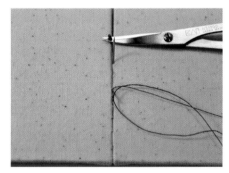

6. Once back at the start, cut the knot off and then continue along the join past the starting stitches until the join can be finished with another holding stitch by repeating steps 1–5 using double or triple length stitch spaces, then cut the thread.

MOUNTING THE EMBROIDERED SECTIONS

There are two traditional methods of mounting your embroideries. The main method used for box-making is lacing (pulling together two edges of fabric with long stitches worked across the two sides) because this method creates less bulk between the inside and outside pieces, allowing them to fit together better. The other, more traditional method requires a layer of calico to be glued to the card; the corners are folded ready to be mitred and the main fabric is then herringbone stitched along all edges to the calico, with the mitred corners completed as the stitching reaches each corner (this is where each edge of the fabric is folded in the corner to create two folds which are then ladder stitched together to create a neat join). This method is rarely used in box-making, except when lacing cannot be worked due to the shape of the card, because the addition of the calico layer and the stitches themselves can add unnecessary bulk to the embroidery which lacing doesn't. The latter technique can also be used to make a soft mounted panel or wall hanging when you would not want the fabric to be stretched over card; natural cotton wadding or a soft cotton interlining can be used in place of card. The two techniques can also be combined: if the interior panel is smaller than the exterior then mitred corners will be required prior to lacing. Depending on how the embroidery is mounted and how it will be attached to the box, some embroideries will need to have mitred corners.

For the two mounting techniques you will need some of these items

- Embroidered fabric
- Conservation card
- Buttonhole thread
- Mellor
- Curved needle
- Pins
- Tape measure
- Calico
- Sateen
- Small fabric or straight embroidery scissors

Hints and tips

When pinning, start with one pin in the middle of each side. Once you are happy with the design placement, place more pins working out from each side of the central pin using the grain line to keep the fabric straight with the edge of the card. A mellor can be used in order to create a neat seam by slipping it under the fold to help smooth out the fabric underneath and correct the position of the fold to be centred in the corner of the card. Mellors can also be used to remove pinholes from the sides of the card by smoothing the fabric threads back into place.

MITRED CORNER

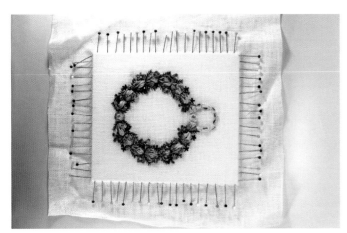

1. Making sure the embroidery is centred on the card, pin the fabric to the edges of the card, making sure to also line up the grain of the fabric with the edge of the card.

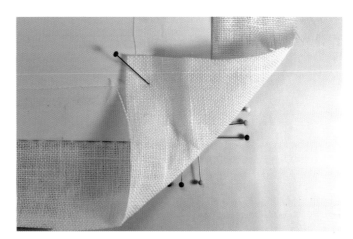

2. Cut the fabric leaving an allowance of approximately 5cm or more around all edges, depending on the lid style, and fold the corner of the fabric over the corner of the card.

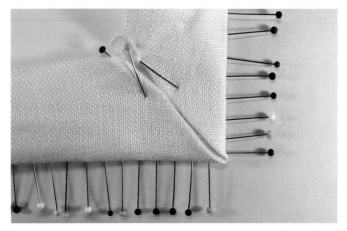

3. Fold over the side edges of the fabric so that the folds meet in the middle, ensuring that the grain remains parallel with the edge, and pin in place.

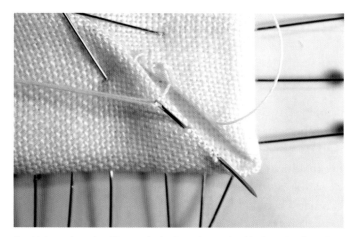

4 Using a length of buttonhole thread or a double length of sewing thread for extra strength, ladder stitch together the seams starting from the interior and working double spaced stitches towards the corner.

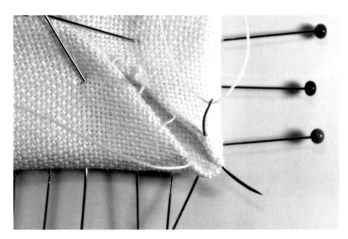

5. For the last stitch before the corner the needle should pass out of the fabric right in the tip of the corner.

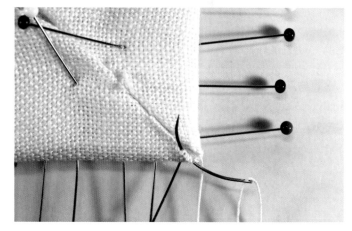

6. In the corner, cross back over to the other side, opposite where the last stitch exits the fabric; this will pull the corner into a nice neat point.

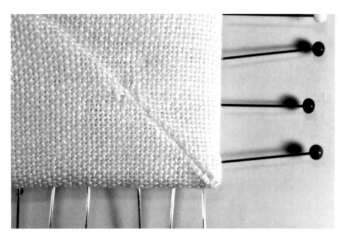

7. Continue back to the first stitch and then the thread can be secured using a holding stitch.

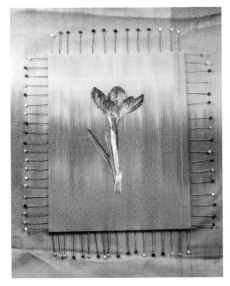

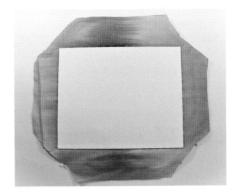

2. Cut diagonally across the corners to remove excess fabric, leaving approximately 1cm of fabric before the corner points.

1. Centre the embroidery on the card panel for the lid and pin into place making sure that any border between the embroidery and the edge of the card is the same measurement for each set of opposite sides.

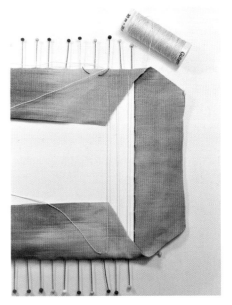

3. Using a curved needle, keeping the thread attached to the spool, within the pinned area, stitch into the fabric carrying the needle under about 5–8mm to form a straight stitch parallel to the edge of the card and pull through a long length of thread. Take the needle over to the opposite side, stitching another straight stitch under the fabric.

4. Continue to alternate between each fabric edge until the lacing stitches reach the other end of the sides being laced together; secure the end of the thread from the needle using a holding stitch.

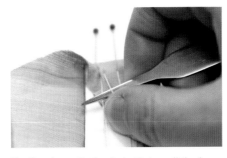

5. Starting with the first stitch, pull the long lengths of thread so that the fabric is pulled taut. A mellor can be used to pull the stitches in order to save your fingers, especially on larger pieces. The fabric may wrinkle slightly between the smaller stitches but this is normal.

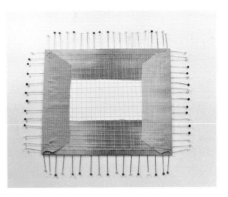

6. Tuck in the corners of the fabric as you fold the two remaining sides over, and repeat steps 3 to 5. Work between the two sides so that all sides of the fabric are laced to their opposing sides, then remove pins from the edge of the card. If the embroidery is going to be framed you can cover the back, following steps 11 to 14 in the traditional mounting instructions given below.

TRADITIONAL MOUNTING

These instructions are for mounting an embroidery to be put in a frame but they can be adapted for use in box-making when lacing can't be used. For example, on the pentagon box in Chapter 6, I had to use herringbone stitch because there was an uneven number of sides making lacing in pairs across the card impossible.

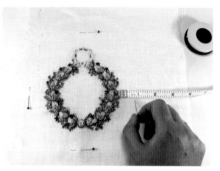

1. Work out the width of the mount that you would like and also the gap that you would like between your embroidery and where the inside of the mount will sit. Place pins in the fabric where the outside edge of the mount will sit.

2. Using the pin markers as a guide, measure the width and length to where the outside edge of the mount will sit.

3. Now using the measurements from between the pins cut out a panel of the conservation card. Place the card on top of the calico (or polycotton if calico will show through the fabric, changing its colour) and cut so it is 2 inches bigger than the card.

4. Put craft glue along the smallest sides but leave about a ½ inch gap from the edge or it will be difficult to stitch into later.

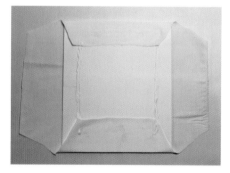

5. Fold the calico over the glue making sure you pull both sides tight to stretch the calico. Cut the corners off the calico, leaving about 1cm of fabric before the corner of the card. Repeat with the longer edges (tuck in the corners in the same way as covering the card with tape) and trim off any excess calico once the glue is dry.

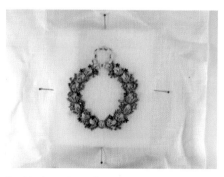

6. Mark on the calico the centre of each edge using a pencil; lay the fabric over the card so that the pins in the fabric line up with the pencil marks so that the design is centred. Make sure that the edges are straight with the edge of the card and that the fabric is flat. Remove the outlining pins from the fabric and push them through the fabric and into the side of the card.

7. Following a grain line along each edge, continue pinning along each of the long sides from the centre out. Now do the same to the smaller two sides, altering the completed sides if necessary to make the grain straight with the edge of the card.

8. The fabric needs to be pulled under tension by removing one pin at a time from the centre of one edge and pulling down a few strands and replacing the pin in the side of the card. Continue on from the middle following the same line from the first adjusted pin; you may wish to add more pins to ensure the edges are straight. Do the same to the opposite side before tightening all the edges until there is no give in the fabric.

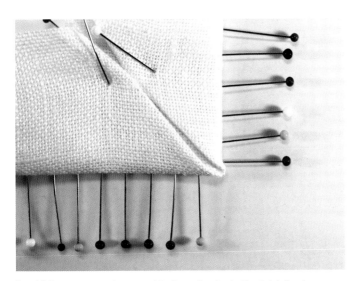

9. All four corners then need to be mitred; pin the folds in place following the mitre instructions in this chapter. The corners will be stitched along with the herringbone stitch (*see* stitch glossary).

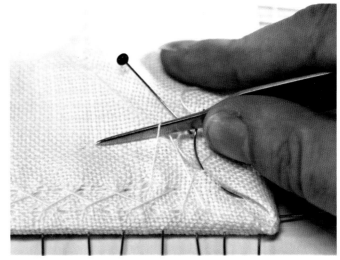

10. Starting from the centre of a side, work herringbone stitch (see Stitch Glossary) along the sides, using a curved needle with buttonhole thread. Stitch the mitred corners together with ladder stitch (see instructions for mitred corners in this chapter). Work your way around the panel making sure that you also catch the calico and the stitches are pulled tight with a mellor before each corner.

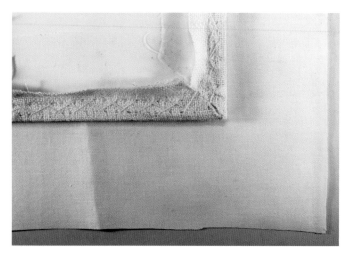

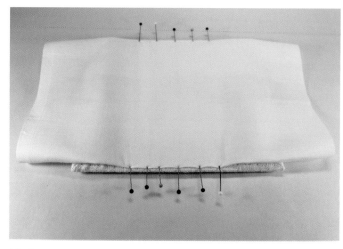

11. Remove the pins, then cut the folds at the corners and trim away any excess to no less than 1cm from the stitching. Cut sateen 2 inches wider than the mounted fabric then place sateen on top of the face-down mounted fabric. The sateen must be shiny side up and the diagonal lines must go from bottom left to top right.

12. Fold one edge of the sateen 2 inches under itself and pin to the back of the panel so that you have a straight edge which is 3mm or so away from the edge of the panel, leaving 2 inches at each end so you can fold back the smaller edges. Now pin the opposite side by folding back the fabric in the same way, making sure the sateen lies straight when you pull it tight.

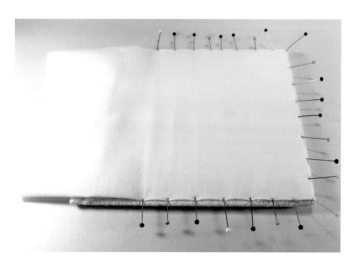

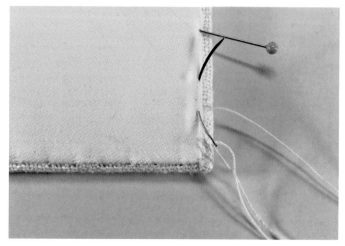

13. Tuck under the first small side using a mellor to straighten the corners if the folded part of the sateen is showing along the edge of the long sides. Again pin from the centre, making sure that the edge is straight and tight. Do exactly the same to the other side, pulling tight, then run a nail along both width and length to test that the tension across the sateen is tight and that it doesn't wrinkle up against your finger; if it does bunch up you will need to tighten.

14. When the sateen is straight and tight you can now ladder stitch around the edges. Start in the centre of a long edge and using a curved needle go back slightly on each stitch (these should be about 4–5mm long) so that when it is pulled tight the stitch does not show. Remove the pins as you go and continue until you have stitched all the way around the sateen.

CORD MAKING

Cords can be made either by hand or using a cord-winding machine; refer to the instructions that are provided, as they may vary slightly. You will need two or three colours of thread (two- or three-ply) from the design you have worked, making sure that at least one of them is a contrasting colour. If you don't have access to a machine, it is possible to wind them by hand. This just takes a bit longer and is easier if you have someone who can help by holding the opposite end of the thread. If you have someone to help you, then tie the thread at each end to a separate pencil (so you may need as many as six pencils, depending on the desired number

of colours). Working with one thread at a time, stand the length of the thread away from each other, each holding one of the pencils. Twist the pencils in opposite directions to twist the thread. Twist each thread until it just starts to twist back on itself when not under tension; you will now be standing closer to your helper. Repeat the process for each thread.

Once all threads have been twisted in this way, the twist direction is switched to twist the threads together. Tie off the cord using a needle to sew around and through it to secure it while keeping it at a tension. Once the cord has been tied off, the pencils can be removed and the cord relaxed ready to use. If you are working alone, you might need to be a bit creative with your set-up! It is possible with shorter

The length of the thread will usually decrease in size by 25cm during the winding process but I would advise allowing at least half a metre on top of the desired length to ensure that you have enough and in case any faults in the twist pattern are created.

lengths of thread to leave the number of strands in one continuous length folded back on itself to make the correct number of strands rather than cutting each strand individually. The step by step photographs show a very small set up to demonstrate how to hand wind a cord. You will usually need a much longer length so may need to place the objects holding the ends of the cord further apart.

1. I tied the cut ends of each thread through bulldog clips, which I attached to a heavy stationery holder. I passed pencils through the loops at the other end of the threads, and wound the threads separately. The pencils for the twisted threads were held in the support for a seat frame, which was weighed down to maintain tension.

2. Each thread was then twisted separately; this can be done by holding the thread close to the pencil in one hand and twisting the pencil in a clockwise direction.

3. I continued twisting each thread until it started to twist back on itself when not under tension. I then secured the twisted thread until all of them had been twisted.

4. I then grouped the threads together and wound them in an anti-clockwise direction again until they were just twisting up when not held under tension.

5. I then placed the pencils into the upright support of a seat frame, which was weighted down with a heavy pestle and mortar to keep it in place; this gave me free hands to tie off the cord.

6. Using a needle and a double length of contrasting thread, I tied off the cord by sewing through and around it several times to prevent it untwisting. Then the pencils were removed and the thread untied from the clips so that the cord relaxed and was ready to use.

·⋅❧[PROJECT]❧·⋅

SMALL GIFT BOX

This small box is great to give as a gift for storing small jewellery items or as a presentation box for a jewellery gift. It is the perfect box for a beginner to learn the basics of box-making because it doesn't require a lot of planning, mathematics or time. This box can be made, once any embroidery is complete, in a day or two.

You will need

- 30cm square of conservation board
- Quilting cotton for the exterior
- Contrasting colour for the interior
- Felt of a sympathetic colour to the exterior fabric
- Sewing thread
- Narrow double-sided tape
- Propelling pencil
- Metal ruler
- Set square
- Stanley knife
- Cutting mat
- Embroidery scissors
- Fine curved needle
- Pins

Heart gift box with surface embroidery stitches.

Hints and tips

You may wish for the interior of the box to be slightly padded. This can be achieved by sticking a layer of felt onto the card with double-sided tape before covering it with fabric. If you can't find a colour of felt to match the fabric perfectly then the nearest sympathetic colour, preferably lighter but not white, is best.

(This is why light grey is used here.) It is always best to start work on the interior panels first so that the measurements for the outer panels can be double-checked before cutting and also as a way of practising the stitch used so it will be as invisible as possible when the box is finished.

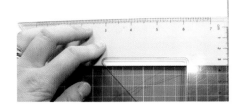

1. Starting with the interior panels, use a metal ruler and a propelling pencil to mark the measurements on the card for the front, back, side and base pieces in a continuous line using the measurements provided. As the measurements will be very similar in size you could mark the squares to remember which is which.

2. Double-check the measurements are correct and make sure that the corners are all at right angles with a set square. When they are all correct carefully cut them out using the Stanley knife and metal ruler; press the knife gently at first so as to avoid slipping. Recheck the sizes when cut and if necessary recut any that are not correct.

3. Using the method shown earlier in this chapter, cover the panels with the interior fabric making sure that the grain and any pattern is running in the same direction and that the fabric is taut enough to be smooth but not stretched.

4. The back and one side panel are stitched together first using ladder stitch. Place the two panels together so that the side panel is butted up against the inside edge of the back panel to create an L shape. Make sure that the fabric side faces inwards and that the panels are the correct way up so they are level at the top and bottom.

5. Starting a new single length of sewing thread, ladder stitch the exterior edge where the two panels meet, starting at either the top or bottom depending on which hand you use to sew with. Finish the thread using holding stitches in an area of fabric at the back where they won't be seen.

6. The joined sides are then placed onto the base and stitched in place, using ladder stitch, so that they can be supported by the base. A small gap should be left at the end of the side piece for the front panel to fit into.

Interior measurements

	Width (cm)	Height (cm)
Front and back panels	4.4	4.1
Side panels (×2)	3.8	4.1
Base panel	4.4	4.4

7. Using a new length of sewing thread, the other side panel can then be attached to the back and base, leaving a gap before the same edge as the first side.

8. The front panel is then ladder stitched in the gap between the two sides, to the base and side panels to finish the interior of the box.

1. Check the measurements for the exterior of the box will remain the same now that the interior has been completed. Then measure and cut the exterior sides, back and front. They should be 6mm larger on the width and 3mm taller on the height measurements. Do not cut the base and lid pieces until the main part of the box has been constructed to ensure a good fit.

2. Cover the exterior panels with the contrasting or patterned fabric using the same method as with the interior panels.

3. Starting with the back and side panels as before, join these using ladder stitch at the side edges with the fabric this time facing out.

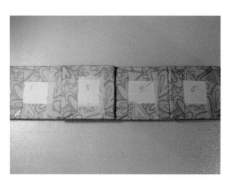

4. Now attach one side of the front panel to one of the side panels leaving the other side open for now so they are all in a long line.

5. Take the interior box and wrap the exterior panels around it, making sure that the interior side panels are next to exterior side panels.

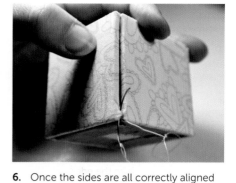

6. Once the sides are all correctly aligned with the top and bottom edges all at the same level, the front section can be ladder stitched closed.

7. Ladder stitch all the way around the top edges of the box so that the interior and exterior panels are jointed together at the top; take care in the corners so that no stitches can be seen where the panels overlap. A ladder holding stitch will need to be used to finish off the thread.

Exterior measurements
(check once interior box has been constructed before cutting)

	Width (cm)	Height (cm)
Front and back panels	5	4.4
Side panels (×2)	4.4	4.4
Base panel	5	5
Interior lid	3.8	3.8
Exterior lid	5	5

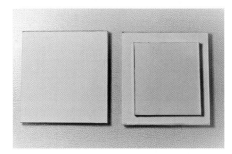

1. Check the final measurements of the box, cut the base and exterior lid to fit over the entire base and top of the constructed box. The interior of the lid should be cut to fit within the internal space of the box.

2. Using double-sided tape, cover the exterior lid panel with felt, following the instructions given earlier in this chapter. Cover the base with the exterior fabric and the interior lid with the interior fabric as with all previous sections. (Also cover the exterior part of the lid if you are leaving it unembroidered.)

3. Ladder stitch the base of the box into place, making sure to hide the starting stitches. To finish the thread, work double stitch length stitches towards the end so that you can turn and work back on the stitches to secure the thread rather than finishing with the small stitches as you did with the previous sides.

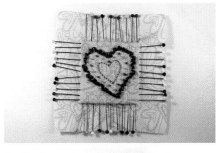

4. Pin the embroidered fabric to the card following the lacing instructions earlier in this chapter. Trim the edges of the fabric back to the top of the pinheads (3–4 cm).

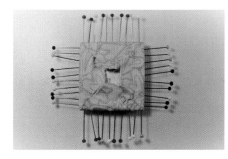

5. Mitre all corners of the exterior lid.

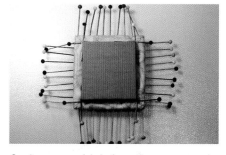

6. Any excess fabric from the corners and the edges can then be trimmed back slightly, making sure that there is enough fabric to lace the sides together. Pins can be placed as a guide for the lacing to be invisible once the interior lid is stitched in place.

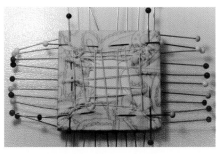

7. Because this is only a small lid, a double length of sewing thread can be used to lace together opposite sides so that all edges of the fabric are secured and the front is taut against the card.

8. Remove the pins from the edge of the card and use a mellor to gently iron out the pinholes from the edges.

9. The inside panel of the lid can then be centred on the back of the exterior lid panel and ladder stitched in place.

CHAPTER 3

LID STYLES

The wide range and variety of possible lid styles is limited only by your imagination and the restrictions of the materials or embroidery you are using. This chapter will guide you through the different lid options and give advice for how the styles in this book can be adapted for use on your own box design. Lids are usually constructed once the rest of the box is complete, but there are a few exceptions; it is also important to consider which style of lid you intend to use before you start constructing the main part of the box, as the lid can affect your decisions on how to construct the entire box. Some of the lids will have more than one option for construction depending on the style and shape of the box that it will fit onto. It is not possible to give step-by-step instructions for every possible variation on each lid type so it is a matter of judgement based on your previous experience.

If you are new to box-making I would recommend constructing a few boxes using the processes shown in this book and adapting just the size to fit your needs before you change the construction process to make a box of your own design. Most techniques of embroidery can be mounted on any box size and shape but it is important to consider the shape of your design, especially if you have already embroidered it, when choosing the style of lid to mount it onto. Small boxes will probably need to be mounted with designs that have been specifically designed for them. Embroidery can also be worked for any of the sides of the box or drawer and cupboard fronts – you are not just restricted to the lid.

Canvas work is best kept restricted to an overlap style of lid because the raw sides of the canvas can be hidden within the sides of the box and the edges covered with cord to give a neat edge. It is possible to use canvas on the sides of a box but you would have decide whether to mount over card (where the extra thickness would need to be added to the measurements) or soft mount. Depending on how well the sides join together you may need to attach a cord, or stitch the sides together with a diagonal stitch to cover any raw canvas.

BOXES WITHOUT LIDS

There will be times when you require a box with a drawer or cupboard door instead of a lid. These can be made in various ways but most involve creating a box structure which will then either be used for a drawer or have a door attached, like a hinged lid. Embroidery can still be mounted on the top and even on the drawer or cupboard door fronts.

Close-up of stumpwork flowers
(Chapter 6).

Padded Lid

Padded lids are constructed from two panels of card joined with wrong sides together. The inside is smaller to fit within the internal space of the box, and a layer of felt or bump is added to the outside to raise the embroidery, giving a rounded appearance to the lid. This is probably the easiest lid type to construct, as it has the smallest number of elements. Any type of fabric can be used on this lid type, apart from leather and canvas. The corners on the back of the top panel have to be mitred to give a neat finish on the inside of the lid; this is not possible with leather because it has to be cut to reduce the bulk. Similarly, canvas is better soft mounted on a box rather than mounted over card, again because of the thickness and stiffness of the material.

Lids on small gift boxes or trinket boxes can be left loose or may be attached to the box to create a hinge. The bottom panel of the lid is cut just allowing room for the fabric to fit into the internal space of the box; the tight fit means that the lid is secure when fitted onto the box base. The embroidered top of the lid is placed over the top of the card with a layer of padding and then the corners are mitred on the reverse prior to lacing the fabric into place.

Padded lid with embroidery stitches and beads (Chapter 2).

Padded lids can be used for boxes of any shape and the instructions given in the previous chapter can be adapted according to the shape of box you require; the construction of the lid will only differ in that the two panels are a different shape. All corners will need to be mitred and the interior panel must be cut just smaller than the internal space of the box, taking into account the thickness of the fabric used.

Hints and tips

You could also use a thin layer of wadding or more than one layer of bump to increase the padding on the lid. If you decide to use wadding, once the layer is cut to the size of the board, trim the sides with fabric scissors at an angle to create a smoother, less hard edge to the padding.

Lid with three angled sides on the men's travel box (Chapter 4).

LIDS WITH ANGLED SIDES

Angled-sides lids are constructed of joined interior and joined exterior panels; the interior panels are constructed first and then the exterior panels before they are joined together. The shape and angle of the two smaller sides is slightly restricted by the card and fabric used; it is not possible to have the angle end in a point on the side, because it is not possible to obtain a neat fold on a small point. Therefore the shape of your lid will be decided partly by how small a panel side you are able to cover comfortably. This is a slightly more complicated lid style to construct because the angles have to be matched from the interior panels and then extended on the exterior panels, which will be bigger to fit over the interior panels.

Like the padded lid, any thinner type of fabric can be used, i.e. not leather or canvas because the angles of the sides are not suited to thick and stiff fabrics. Thicker fabric will make it harder (but not impossible) to match the correct angle on the exterior to that of the interior.

The lid from the box in Chapter 4 (above) only has three sides in order to create a hinge to join it to the box and make it more secure. This style of lid can be adapted for various sized and shaped boxes (except circular boxes). Many of the sides around the top embroidered panel can be angled (or shaped) as long as one edge on the top embroidered panel is left without a side panel to create a hinge on. For example, a pentagon box has five sides, but only four would have angled side panels (the interior top panel

Hints and tips

This style of lid can also be adapted and constructed in a similar way to an overlap lid with the sides angled to a point in the centre of each panel rather than from one end to the other. This would be suitable for boxes with more than four sides.

is extended on that one side so that it ends flush with the exterior panel) so that the fifth side can be left empty to create a hinge between the lid and the box. This style of lid is perfect for smaller trinket or jewellery boxes but can also be used for a more modern-looking sewing box, larger jewellery box or for keepsakes.

Hinge lid with crewelwork from the charm box (Chapter 4).

Hinge lid

Hinge lids are constructed in a similar way to padded lids, either using a single layer of card with the backing mounted in the same way as if you were mounting a piece for a frame (see mounting instructions in Chapter 2) or they can also be constructed from two panels of card which are joined wrong sides together, the inside being smaller to fit within the internal space of the box. Both methods of lid construction are then stitched along the back edge to the box base to form a hinged opening.

Any fabric can be used for this lid, even canvas and leather should you wish, but the construction will need to be adapted slightly. Because only one layer of card is likely to be used a slightly thicker fabric is more suited to this style of lid. The thickness of the fabric needs to be taken into account by reducing the size of the card panel by the thickness of the fabric on all sides.

This style of lid can be adapted for use on any size and shape of box except circular boxes. It is particularly suited for boxes that have dividers for jewellery (like the charm box in Chapter 4), sewing boxes, or boxes for keepsakes or even toys. You may wish the dividers to be the same height as the sides of the box rather than leaving a small gap for the inside part of the lid to fit into.

This lid style could be combined with the padded lid using foam pads and MDF to create a seat storage box for toys or blankets and other items for a living room or bedroom. The same principles are used no matter what size box you are creating; the materials just need to be adapted so that they are strong enough for the desired use.

Hints and tips

If using leather or canvas for this lid style, you will need to carry the backing fabric right to the edges of the lid rather than leaving a small gap as you would with other mounted pieces. I would recommend stitching a canvas design larger than the desired lid of the box so that it is carried around to the back. If you are using leather, try to cut the corners so that they sit slightly in from the corner of the card so that it can be hidden behind the backing.

Overlap lid with canvas work from the etui box (Chapter 5).

OVERLAP LID

Overlap lids are constructed from joined interior panels and joined exterior panels, the number of which depends on the shape of the box, which are then joined together to make a single lid which sits snugly over the sides of the box. This is constructed in a similar way to the main part of the box but it has narrower sides to make a clear distinction from the main part of the box.

This style of lid can be adapted for use with any box shape and size but it is particularly well suited to larger, deeper boxes, especially if they have a lift-out tray, as the lid can be removed completely rather than being attached to the side. They can be used for hat, fascinator or tiara storage boxes, keepsake/memory boxes and are used for etui boxes, where the box sides are not joined and the lid holds the box together.

The step-by-step method used for the construction of this lid type is slightly different from how it would usually be constructed for a box with all sides joined together, as all interior and exterior panels would usually be constructed with card. Due to the use of canvas embroidery on the lid I have constructed for the etui box in Chapter 5, I have made some minor changes to the construction (this is a good example of how the lid construction can easily be changed to suit any type of embroidery or box). This was the most suitable lid type for canvas embroidery due to the thickness of the canvas and to prevent the canvas from showing.

Any thickness of fabric can be used on this style of lid but thicker fabrics will need to be taken into account when working out the sizes of the panels. This lid style can also be combined with the padded lid to give a slightly raised top panel. This is particularly necessary if you are using an embroidery technique where the reverse of the embroidery may be a bit uneven, such as ribbonwork (although this can be avoided by securing the thread rather than using knots on the back) or goldwork, which has plunged threads.

Fitted lid with stumpwork from the bracelet box (Chapter 6).

FITTED LID

Fitted lids are constructed in a similar way to the overlap lid but the interior panels of the lid will be either shorter or longer than the exterior panels so that the exterior lid sits flush with the sides of the main box rather than overlapping. The inside panels of the box will be the opposite of the lid, depending on how you wish the lid to fit onto the main part of the box. The lid exterior can be the same size as the exterior of the main part of the box or it can be larger or smaller than the main box section.

This style of lid can be used for any size and shape of box and works particularly well with circular boxes, as shown in the step-by-step guide in Chapter 6. If used on a box with more than one side the construction is very similar to that of a circle but is combined with the construction method used for an overlap lid. The most important thing to remember is that where the interior panels are either shorter or longer than the exterior, any interior or exterior sections that will be visible will need to have mitred corners so that they are neatly finished.

Any thickness of fabric can be used on this style of lid but thicker fabrics will need to be taken into account when working out the sizes of the panels. Thinner fabrics with a small amount of stretch are ideal for circular lids. This lid style can also be combined with the padded lid to give a slightly raised top panel.

Lift-out lid with goldwork from the memory box (Chapter 6).

LIFT-OUT LID

Lift-out lids are similar to padded lids but the interior panel is the same size as the exterior panel and the exterior sides of the box are extended to cover the sides of the lid so that it rests on the interior side panels and can be lifted out of the box. A ribbon tab is secured between the two panels of the lid so that it can be lifted out.

This lid style is suitable for use with any size and shape of box as it lifts out rather than being secured with a hinge or side panels attached to the lid. It is most suited for boxes that are constructed with multiple openings for storing keepsakes, small pieces of jewellery or even small craft items such as buttons, ribbons or sewing equipment. Boxes with multiple sides are also ideally suited to this style of lid: since it is constructed using two identically sized panels, it is easier to achieve the correct fit.

Thicker fabric can be used on this style of lid should you wish but the thickness of the fabric will need to be taken into account when cutting the panels to ensure ease of fit within the sides of the box. This lid style can be combined with the padded lid to give a domed look or the embroidery can be mounted straight over the card.

Chest lids are constructed using a thinner card than other lids in order to create a curve over the depth of the box base. Two part-circle panels are cut, either half or less than half, to be fitted to the sides, and a panel is cut to fit within the inside opening. Lids with sides are usually constructed from interior and exterior sections joined together but a chest lid has a hollow centre to hide the lacing from the embroidery (this also helps the lid to keep its curved shape).

Lids of this style can be worked on any size of box but are only suitable for use on square or rectangular boxes. The advantage of having a hollow space behind the interior panel is that an opening can be made in the centre for a mirror to be attached behind. Mirrors are reasonably thick so this is the most suitable lid type for them to be used with. It is still possible to mount them in other lids but extra card would be needed to pack out the lid in order for the mirror to be secured while maintaining the correct shape.

This lid style can be adapted to create a roof lid; this would have two panels forming a pointed roof with triangular panels at each side rather than a curved top and circular sides. The method for joining the two angled sides will depend on the angle; you may wish to add a cord along the top edge to conceal the join, especially if it is not overlapping.

Chest lid with smocking from the travel jewellery box (Chapter 7).

Any fabric, except for leather on the chest lid, would be suitable for this lid type. Fabric with a slight stretch would be ideal for the chest lid but is not essential. Because the chest lid is curved and therefore needs a thinner card, I would avoid using an embroidery technique that requires a very strong tension when mounted, because the fabric will not be mounted quite as tightly as other lids due to the card bending. The roof lid has no such restrictions.

Hints and tips

A roof lid could be used to create a box that looks like a shed or cottage or even a fantasy house. The chest lid would be ideal for a pirate's treasure chest, with a false panel decorated with coins hiding the real treasure stored below.

Two-colour lid with goldwork and ribbonwork from the large jewellery box (Chapter 10).

TWO-COLOUR LID

Two-colour lids are a cross between padded, overlap and fitted lid types. The interior part of the lid is larger than the exterior with the mitred corners visible on the exterior of the lid. The exterior and embroidered part of the lid is then mounted centrally on top of the interior panel with the corners lining up with the mitred corner joins. The lid can be mounted as a flat panel or it can have a ring of joined interior and exterior side panels attached to the bottom of the interior lid panel. This would sit flush with the sides of the box in order to add height to the lid, if there is a ring holder in the section below the lid, for example.

Lids of this style are more suited to medium and large boxes: the space of the embroidery is made smaller because the interior fabric creates a frame around the central embroidered panel. The lid could be adapted, by an experienced maker, so that rather than the interior panel being larger, strips with angled ends (rather than straight) could be cut for the sides to create a bevelled effect for the central panel to be set into. This would require a lot of testing in advance to achieve the correct fit for both the interior and exterior panels.

Any fabric can be used for this lid with the exception of leather – the angle of the needle needed to join the interior and exterior lid panel would make sewing a very stiff fabric even harder. The exterior lid panel can be padded with felt or bump, or can be left unpadded depending on the embroidery.

CHAPTER 4

TRAYS, DRAWERS, STACKING BOXES AND DIVIDERS

Boxes are not limited to being constructed with one internal space and a lid: there are endless possibilities that can be created to fit within the box depending on your needs. Lift-out trays, drawers, stacking boxes and dividers can all be incorporated into your design. This chapter will guide you through the process of constructing these additions to your box as well as providing design ideas. All instructions are guidelines only; as you gain more experience and understand the process of construction you will be able to make changes to fit the requirements of your box.

Lift-out trays are useful for storing small sets of jewellery for travel and they can be included in larger boxes to save space, rather than keeping items in their original boxes. They can also be used for storing threads and smaller pieces of needlework equipment as well as make-up and hair accessories. Lift-out trays can be made to fit within any size and shape of box, and it is even possible to create two trays to sit side by side as long as there are enough supports in place to keep them at the cor-

Stacking charm jewellery box with dividers for unworn charms.

rect level in the box. A tray can also be designed to sit within a small section of the box if you need extra height in one section of the box for larger items.

When constructing trays that will sit inside a box it is advisable to construct the tray first and then the box, to ensure that all parts will fit correctly. This is because the measurements can sometimes change slightly – no matter how detailed your design plan. The same principle applies to drawers and dividers: they are constructed individually first and then the casing or trays are created to fit around them.

Drawers can be designed as stand-alone units or be part of a larger box design; the drawer that I have designed for this chapter is designed to sit on a bedside table for keeping glasses, a watch and to hide a phone at night while it's charging. The advantage of having a drawer rather than a lid is that it can be left slightly open for the cable and closed fully during the day; the drawer won't need to be fully removed from the surround but a lid would have to be placed elsewhere or have a hinge with supports. Drawers are particularly useful on boxes with multiple layers, as it is easier to access a drawer at the bottom of the

box than it is to remove a series of trays to access the items at the bottom. You can also add dividers within the drawer to separate out the items.

Stacking boxes are particularly useful if you are likely to add to the collection of items you are storing; you can make a new one when you require more space rather than having to design a whole new box. If you wish to use the same fabric it is important to make sure that you have more than enough to make the extra trays you might require at a later date. Also, make sure that you keep a record of the measurements you have used for each element of the trays so that it is possible to replicate them exactly.

Dividers are a great way of customizing your box or tray to fit perfectly around the items you wish to store and keep separate from other items. This is particularly useful when storing smaller items that are easily tangled, such as jewellery. When combined with stacking boxes they are perfect for storing charms: you might not wish to have them all on the necklace or bracelet at once and by making the boxes stacking it is easy to make another tray to keep them all together but in their own separate space.

MEN'S LEATHER TRAVEL JEWELLERY BOX WITH TRAY

Men's leather cufflink and tie-clip box with monogram of three initials GJB.

You will need

- Conservation board
- Leather/suede for the exterior, 1mm thick or less (antique leather was used for this box)
- Fat quarter of silk for the interior and lid
- Sewing and buttonhole thread
- Ribbon for tray pulls
- Round-nose pliers
- Narrow double-sided tape

- Propelling pencil
- Metal ruler
- Set square
- Stanley knife
- Cutting mat
- Embroidery and fabric scissors
- Fine curved needle
- Pins

Hints and tips

When considering the size of your box it is important to allow extra width to the main box sides in order for the tray to be easily removed from the box. Also allow extra space on all sides of the tray and the inside of the box to ensure easy removal of the items stored within.

CONSTRUCTING THE TRAY

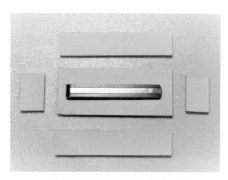

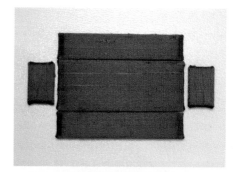

1. Measure the tie clip and cut out a base and four sides. The side panels, which are all the same height, sit on top of the base so the base needs to be 6mm bigger on the depth and width than the area needed to hold the tie clip. The shorter side panels sit between the long side panels, so they will need to be 6mm shorter than the base depth to allow for the thickness of the panels when covered.

2. Using double-sided tape, stick felt to the pieces of card, leaving a 2mm gap at each end of the long side panels and all the way around the base edges.

3. Cover all interior tray panels in the interior silk fabric using the double-sided tape method set out in Chapter 2.

4. Because the panels are very small, start by joining one of the long side panels to the base using ladder stitch; this will make attaching the smaller panels easier.

5. Placing the short side panel so that it sits against the inside edge of the long side panel, attach the short side panel to both joined panels using ladder stitch.

6. Attach the second long side to the base and short side panel using ladder stitch. Then attach the other short side panel between the two long side panels to complete the interior part of the tray.

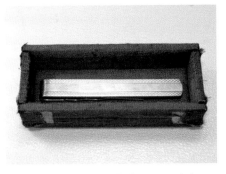

7. Check that the tie clip fits correctly in the interior part of the tray.

8. Then attach a small folded piece of satin ribbon in the middle of each short side panel of the tray, stitching through the ribbon to secure it.

9. Check the interior tray measurements and cut out exterior side panels, which should be about 5–6mm wider and 2–3mm higher than the interior tray panels. A base can also be cut which will be 5–6mm wider and deeper than the interior base panel.

10. Cover the exterior tray panels in the same way as the interior tray panels, again using the interior silk fabric.

11. With the fabric facing outwards place one short side panel against the back of a long side panel and secure using ladder stitch.

12. Join the remaining long side panel, with the fabric facing outwards, to the short side panel so that it is parallel to the first long side.

13. Join the remaining short side panel to one long side panel and then wrap the line of joined panels around the interior part of the tray before securing the final corner.

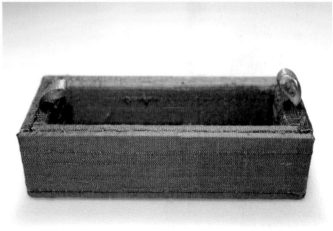

14. Ladder stitch between the interior and exterior tray panels on the top edge to join them together, sewing through the ribbon to hold it in the correct position and being careful as you join the corners.

15. Finally ladder stitch the base onto the bottom of the tray.

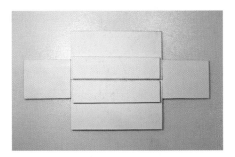

1. Check the final measurements of the tray and cut two of each of the following: tray supports (height of cufflinks plus 2–5mm by length of tray plus 1–2mm); long interior side panels (length of tray supports plus 5–6mm by combined height of tray and tray supports plus 1–2mm); short interior side panels (height of long sides by width of tray plus 1–2mm).

2. Cover all supports and side panels with the interior silk fabric using the double-sided tape method described in Chapter 2.

3. Place the tray supports so that each one is centred on a long side panel; there will be a 2–3mm gap each end of the support for the short side panels to fit into. With the bottoms of each panel level, ladder stitch around the edges of each tray support, joining them to the long sides.

4. Join a short side panel to the inside edge of one long side panel with the fabric facing inwards so that the short side also sits against the edge of the tray support.

5. Join the second short side panel to the other end of the long side panel, using ladder stitch.

6. Join the remaining long side panel to both of the short side panels to create a rectangle.

7. Check that the tray fits within the interior box and can also be easily removed.

8. Measure the width and length of the interior box sides and cut a base that is 1mm shorter on the width and length to allow for the fabric. Cover with the interior silk fabric.

9. Using ladder stitch, attach the interior base to the interior box on all sides.

Leather is a much thicker and stiffer material to deal with than other fabrics; if you wish you can construct the exterior of this box with other fabrics. If you do wish to use leather then please use this next set of instructions as a guide only. When cutting the exterior sides you will need to take into account the thickness of the leather; for instance, if the leather is 1mm thick then an extra allowance of 2mm (leather allowance) will need to be taken off the length and width of the card, on top of the usual allowance for the thickness of the card. The corners of the leather will be secured using a similar technique to the usual method of mitring; this can be adapted where necessary. The thimble and round-nose pliers will be necessary to sew through the leather without getting sore fingers.

1. Starting with the small side panels first, measure the interior sides of the box and take only the leather allowance off the height and width measurements. Using fabric scissors cut out a piece of leather for each side panel with an allowance of 1–1.5cm and cut off the corners, leaving an allowance of no less than 5mm. Stick double-sided tape to all edges of the card.

2. Place the leather so that the suede side is on the outside, and fold over the edges of the leather onto the tape. With a fine pair of scissors trim the leather back so that each flap lies flat with no overlaps, making sure that there is enough left in the corners to cover the card.

3. Using a single strand of sewing thread in a curved needle and the round-nose pliers, sew the corner into a mitre. Start with a knot on the back of the leather and sew through the edge on the opposite side to the starting knot.

4. Once the two edges have been pulled together, if needed small notches can be snipped off the leather between the stitch and the corner.

5. Then take the needle and, sewing from the leather to suede side, stitch to the corner point and then back to the first stitch, pulling the corner in tightly.

6. Do the same with the left side of the corner, again pulling it back tightly to the first stitch.

7. The centre of the corner then needs to be tightly pulled in so that once the side is attached the corners will not be visible. The thread can then be secured to the existing stitches.

8. Repeat the above method for all remaining corners on the two small side pieces.

9. Both short side panels then need to be attached to the interior section short side panels of the box using ladder stitch. Take care on the corners to make sure that any cut edges of the leather are hidden against the interior box side panels.

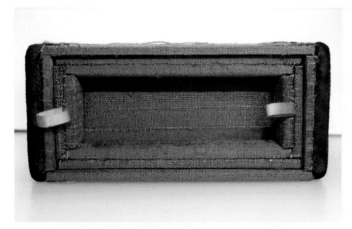

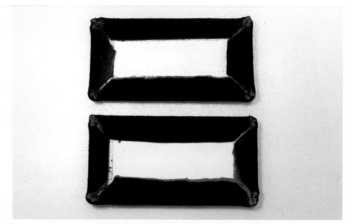

10. Now the short ends are in place, measure the long sides of the box. Once again taking off the leather allowance from the height and width, cut two pieces of card for the long sides.

11. Cover the large side panels using the same method as for the short side panels (steps 2–8).

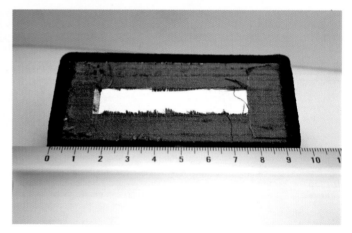

12. Using ladder stitch, attach both the long side panels to the box, securing on all sides to the interior long side panels and exterior short side panels.

13. Now the long ends are in place, measure the base of the box and, again taking off the leather allowance from the height and width, cut one piece of card for the base.

14. Cover the base using the same method as for the other sides (steps 2–8).

15. Using ladder stitch with the round-nose pliers, attach the base to the box, securing on all sides to the exterior sides.

1. Measure the finished dimensions of the box and, allowing 2–3mm extra for ease of fit, cut and cover an interior lid top with the silk.

2. The interior front and side lid panels will then need to be cut to sit within the edges of the interior top. The front panel should be the same length as the top and the depth should increase by 5mm or more so that it is deeper in the middle. The sides should be the width of the top minus the thickness of the front (2–3mm); the sides should be the same depth where they join the front and then taper to no less than 7mm at the back edge.

3. The side panels need to be joined using ladder stitch to both ends of the front panel with the fabric facing inwards.

4. The joined front and side panels can then be ladder stitched to the interior top starting on one of the smaller sides; the fabric should face inwards.

5. After checking the finished measurements of the interior side panels, cut out the card for the two shorter exterior panels. The height must remain the same as the interior sides and the depth of the top panel. The width should be increased to fit in line with the interior panels (interior sides and depth of front interior panel); cover with the silk fabric.

6. Then use ladder stitch to secure all edges of each exterior side panel to each interior side panel of the lid with the fabric facing outwards.

7. After checking the length and depth of the front panel cut out the exterior front so that it is flush with all edges. Then cover with the silk and secure on all edges to the constructed lid using ladder stitch.

8. After checking the final measurements for the exterior lid, cut out a panel of card, cover with a layer of felt and mount the embroidery using the lacing method as described in Chapter 2.

9. Once your embroidery has been securely mounted onto the card it can then be stitched along all edges onto the top of the lid using ladder stitch.

10. Place the completed lid onto the finished box and use ladder stitch, starting and finishing with a ladder holding stitch, to create a hinge for the lid by joining the silk and leather edges together where they meet.

BEDSIDE STORAGE DRAWER

Bedside storage drawer with silk shaded crocus.

You will need

- Conservation board
- Cotton fabric for interior
- Cotton fabric for exterior (an ikat-style fabric has been used for this project)
- Sewing and buttonhole thread
- Large and small bead for drawer pull (can be matching or contrasting)
- Stiletto
- Narrow double-sided tape
- Propelling pencil
- Metal ruler
- Set square
- Stanley knife
- Cutting mat
- Embroidery and fabric scissors
- Fine curved needle
- Pins
- Bulldog clips
- Clear craft glue
- Printer paper

1. Measure the objects that you wish to store in the drawer and add 1–2cm to the final size to allow them to be easily removed. Cut out a base, a front and back the same width as the base edge it will sit on, and two sides which will be the base length minus 5–6mm to allow for the front and back card and fabric thickness. Cover all pieces of card with the interior drawer fabric.

3. Line up the joined panels with the base. The end of the longer side panel should sit before the end of the base, leaving a gap for the back to sit in. Stitch both panels into place to join them to the base.

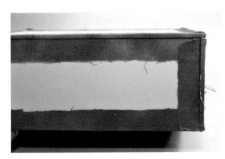

5. To complete the interior part of the drawer, place the remaining long side panel between the front and back side panels and secure on all three edges.

2. Place a drawer front onto the covered end of one of the side pieces so that the wrong side is facing out and stitch into place using ladder stitch.

4. Place the back panel onto the base and secure it where it joins to the long side panel and then along the base.

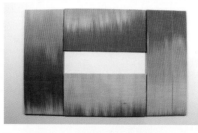

1. Measure the interior drawer exterior to check how much the fabric thickness has affected the size and cut the exterior front, back and side panels. All side panels should be 5–6mm bigger than the same interior panels to take into account the thickness of the covered card.

2. Cut and cover all the panels in the exterior fabric, trying to keep the flow of the fabric's colour pattern where possible so that the fabric changes from light to dark from the front to the back.

3. Use a tape measure to work out the centre point of the drawer front (this can be marked with a temporary pin) and then using a stiletto push down through the fabric and the card. Carefully place two of your fingers either side of the centre at the back to stabilize the card and push the stiletto (twisting if necessary) to form a hole through the card. Once the stiletto has pierced though the back of the card it can be inserted into the hole from the back in order to create an evenly sized hole.

4. Thread up an embroidery needle, big enough to hold the thread but small enough to fit through both beads, with three long strands of sewing thread doubled over so that there are six strands in the needle and a loop at the other end. Thread the larger bead and then the smaller bead onto the needle and push them down onto the thread; place a finger through the loop to stop them sliding off.

5. Pass the needle back through the larger of the two beads so that the small bead acts as a lock to hold the larger bead on the thread.

6. Thread both ends of the thread onto the needle and insert it into the hole in the drawer front created by the stiletto. Then, with two fingers either side of the hole, pull the thread through to the other side so that the large bead is flat against the drawer front.

7. Tie the two ends of the thread together to create a large knot on the back of the card.

8. Using small bulldog clips, secure the end of the thread at opposite ends of the drawer front (a scrap piece of fabric can be used to protect the fabric from the clips). Place a small amount of glue onto the thread near the knot and cover with a small strip of paper. This will ensure that the threads will not come loose when the bead is pulled to open the drawer. Any excess glue should be wiped off with a tissue. Leave to dry for a few hours depending on the glue used and then trim back the thread to the paper strip.

1. Place the exterior long side panel against the drawer front panel with the fabric facing outwards and join the two sections together using ladder stitch.

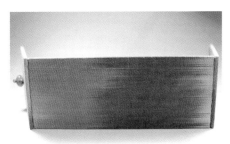

2. Place the exterior back panel of the drawer against the other end of the exterior side panel and join together using ladder stitch.

3. Place the remaining exterior long side panel against the exterior back panel of the drawer and join only to the back panel using ladder stitch.

4. Place the constructed interior part of the drawer in the middle of the exterior panels and wrap them closely around. Using ladder stitch, secure the long exterior side panel to the drawer front and then continue to stitch all the way around the top edge to join the interior and exterior panels together.

5. Measure the base of the drawer to double-check the final measurements and then cut and cover a panel of card for the drawer base, where possible keeping continuity of pattern on the fabric.

6. Using ladder stitch, join the base panel onto the bottom of the drawer.

1. Using the final measurements of the drawer, cut top and base panels 6–8mm wider than the width of the drawer and 4mm longer (depending on the card/fabric thickness). Then cut two long side panels to the same length as the top/base pieces and 1–2mm bigger than the height of the drawer (to allow for ease of removal). Finally, cut one back panel the same height as the long side panels and the width of the top/base panels minus 6mm to allow for the thickness of the sides; cover all panels with the exterior fabric.

2. Start by joining the back panel to one of the long side panels, using ladder stitch. The fabric should be facing inwards and the back panel should be sitting level with the end of the long side panel.

3. Place the joined back and side panels onto the base panel and secure in place using ladder stitch. There should be a small gap left at the end of the back panel for the remaining long side panel to fit into.

4. Place the remaining long side panel onto the base panel and join, starting at the top of the long side panel, working along the base panel and then up the edge of the back panel, using ladder stitch.

5. Place the top panel of the drawer casing onto the joined long side panels and back panel; secure to all three sections using ladder stitch.

6. Place the drawer inside the interior part of the drawer casing to check that it can be removed smoothly before continuing. Make any adjustments if necessary.

7. Cut and cover two exterior side panels and an exterior back panel. All three pieces should be the same height as the completed interior casing sections. The two long side panels should be 3mm longer and the back panel should be 6mm wider to make it the same width as the completed interior back panel (depending on the thickness of the card/fabric).

8. With the fabric facing outwards, join one of the long side panels to the back panel so that the back is flush with the end of the long side panel, using ladder stitch.

9. Join the remaining long side panel to the other end of the back panel, making sure that the back is flush with the end of the long side panel.

10. Wrap the exterior sides and back piece around the interior part of the drawer casing and secure the long ends to their interior counterparts on the outside edges only.

11. Check the measurements of the completed parts of the drawer casing and cut the card panels for the exterior top and base. Cover only the base panel and then using ladder stitch, secure all four sides of the exterior base panel to the edges of the drawer casing.

12. Take the exterior top panel of card and, following the lacing instructions in Chapter 2, lace the embroidery onto the exterior top section without padding.

13. Place the mounted embroidery on the top of the drawer casing and secure on all sides using ladder stitch to complete the drawer casing.

STACKING CHARM JEWELLERY BOX WITH DIVIDERS

You will need

- Conservation board
- Cotton fabric for interior
- Printed cotton fabric for exterior
- Sewing and buttonhole thread
- Narrow double-sided tape
- Propelling pencil
- Metal ruler
- Set square
- Stanley knife
- Cutting mat
- Embroidery and fabric scissors
- Fine curved needle
- Pins
- Felt to match both fabrics

CONSTRUCTING THE INTERNAL DIVIDERS

Measure the bracelet to be stored in the top tray to work out the dimensions for the larger section and allow a little extra space each side. The smaller sections have the same total size as the larger section but it is divided into four smaller boxes for extra charms to be stored. All interior pieces will have the same height measurement. Also measure the necklace for the bottom tray to ensure that the overall size for the top tray will also fit the necklace. The same measurements are used for both trays, just adapted depending on whether the tray has dividers or not.

Crewelwork box for bracelet, necklace and charm storage with dividing sections.

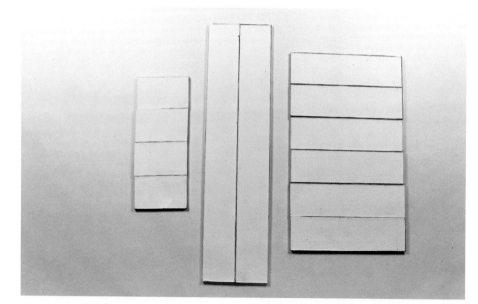

1. Cut two interior long side panels, which are the length of the two interior storage sections combined. Cut out six width panels; these will be the finished width of the internal tray minus 6mm for the thickness of the long sides. Then cut out four mini dividers; these divide the width sections in half to create the mini boxes and should be half the size of the width dividers minus 6mm because there are two panels of card for each width divider.

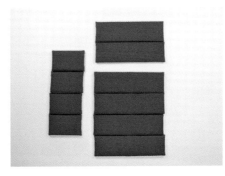

2. Put the long side panels to one side and cover all the width panels and the mini dividers with felt a similar colour to the interior fabric. Two of the width dividers should be covered in their entirety for the sides of the bracelet section. The remaining four divider panels should have two felt pieces, which are the same size as the mini dividers, so that there is a gap left in the middle for the mini dividers to fit into (approximately 6mm).

3. Cover all the width and mini dividers with the interior fabric.

4. The two sets of mini dividers are joined together first, by placing the wrong sides together and ladder stitching around all edges.

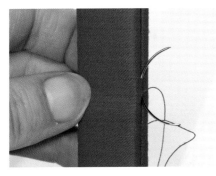

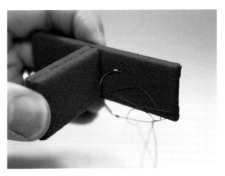

5. Two sets of the width dividers are then joined together. The first pair should have a width panel fully covered with felt on one side and the other side should be one of the width dividers with a gap in the middle of the felt. The other pair should both be width dividers with a gap in the middle of the felt. These are joined on all sides with ladder stitch like the mini dividers.

6. The two remaining width dividers, one with and one without a gap in the felt, now become the outer side panels of the interior tray. Put the one without a gap in the felt to one side so that it is not mixed up with the others. Set out the dividers so they are in the correct order; from left to right the pair with one full length of felt is placed with the felt gap facing towards the right. Then place a mini divider across the middle, followed by the width divider with the double felt gap, the other mini divider next and then the single piece with a gap in the felt placed on the end facing inwards.

7. Place the single side against a mini divider so that it fits within the gap in the felt. Using ladder stitch, join the mini divider to the side panel by stitching all the way around the two end sections of the mini divider, making sure that it is square with the side panel.

9. The second mini divider is then joined (using ladder stitch) onto the other side of the first double width divider, taking care to make sure that it is straight.

10. The last double width divider is then joined (using ladder stitch) to the other side of the second mini divider to complete the dividing section, taking care to make sure that it is straight.

8. The first of the double width dividers is then joined (using ladder stitch) to the other end of the first mini divider, in the same way as the single panel, again taking care to make sure that it is straight.

11. The long side panels now need to be covered completely on one side with felt and then covered with the interior fabric.

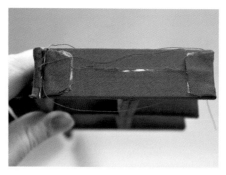

12. Place one of the long side panels against the dividers so that the single side panel's end is flush with the end of the long side, and join the two together using ladder stitch.

13. The width dividers both need to be joined to the long end to stop them from moving. Check the spacing between them to make sure that they are evenly spaced before securing the top and bottom of each end to the long edge using small ladder stitches.

14. The last single side panel (that was put to one side) can then be joined on the other end of the long side panel, using ladder stitch.

15. The second long side panel can then be joined to the other side of the two single side panels, using ladder stitch to join each end in the corners.

16. Then, checking that the spacing for the width dividers is the same as the opposite side, secure the top and bottom of each width divider end to the remaining long side panel.

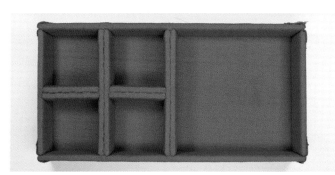

17. Check the final measurements of the divider sections and then cut a base to cover the entire bottom of the divider sections in one piece so that all edges sit flush with the sides. Cover the entire top section of the base in the same colour felt as used on the dividers.

18. Cover the base panel with the interior fabric; place the dividing sections on the base panel so that the sides are flush with the edge of the base, and join together using ladder stitch.

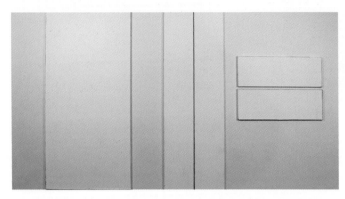

1. Using the same measurements for the interior base panel, cut another panel for the exterior base. Cut two exterior long side panels 6mm longer than the interior long side panels and two exterior short side panels the same length as the width of the interior divider tray; all panels should be 3mm taller than the final height of the constructed interior tray.

2. The base and side panels can then be covered with the exterior fabric. It is very important to mitre the two corners on the top edge of the sides because they will sit slightly above the interior sections (see instructions in Chapter 2). The main length of the fabric can be secured using tape and the corners folded in before sewing together to form the mitred corner. The bottom edge can be folded and then secured using the tape method.

3. With the exterior fabric facing outwards and the mitred corners at the top, join one of the shorter sides to a long side so that the short side sits flush with the end of the long side.

4. Place the joined exterior side against a short interior side so that the unjoined end is flush with the long side. Using ladder stitch along the edge of the interior side, join the exterior to the interior panels.

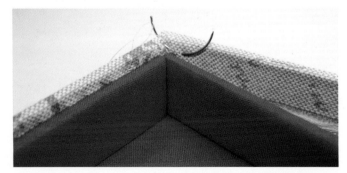

5. Pass the thread over to the long side before pressing it against the interior long side and continuing to stitch along the long side for ease.

6. With the exterior fabric facing outwards and the mitred corners at the top, join the remaining shorter side panel to the remaining long side panel so that the short side sits flush with the end of the long side, making sure that they are joined in the opposite way compared to the first set of joined side panels.

7. The remaining small side panel is then joined onto the interior divider section using ladder stitch, loosely at first along the interior side, then pulling the stitches tight. Leave the corner to join later.

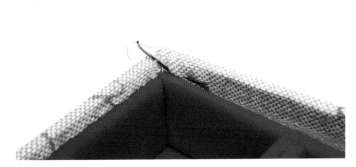

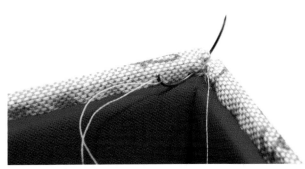

8. As with the first pair of sides, pass the thread over to the long side panel before pressing it against the interior long side panel and continuing to join the two panels together.

9. When back to the first set of joined sides, pass the thread from the second long side panel into the corner and join the exterior side panels together in the corner.

10. The remaining unjoined corners can now be joined together using ladder stitch.

11. The base panel can then be placed on the bottom of the box and joined to the inner edges of the exterior side panels. This creates a slight step between the sides and the base so that when the box is stacked the exterior base sits within the lower tray.

Constructing the Necklace Base Tray

1. Using the same measurements from the top tray for the interior base panel, two width dividers and the long side panels, cut and cover all panels of card fully on one side in felt.

2. Cover all of the felt-lined panels with the interior fabric.

3. Join one of the width side panels to a long side panel (using ladder stitch) with the right side facing inwards so the short side panel sits flush with the end of the long side panel.

4. Starting the thread on the long side panel, stitch the joined sides to the base panel, making sure that a gap is left at the end of the short side for the remaining long side panel to fit into.

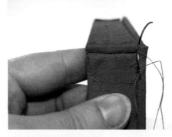

5. Join the remaining long side panel onto the base panel starting in the corner by joining it to the short side panel.

6. The remaining short side can then be joined, starting by stitching down one corner join, working along the base and back up the remaining corner join to complete the interior.

7. Repeat all steps in the earlier instructions for the top tray, constructing the exterior of the tray, as the instructions are the same for this tray.

1. Measure the finished tray you wish to attach the lid to and cut out a piece of card 2mm smaller on both the length and width measurements and cover one side fully with felt.

2. Pin the embroidery to the lid panel making sure that the design is centred with the same measurement on each opposite set of sides and that the grain of the fabric is straight with the edge of the card; trim back the excess fabric so that it is just above the height of the pins.

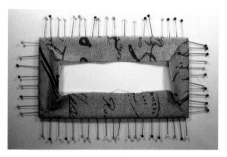

3. Mitre the four corners following the instructions in Chapter 2.

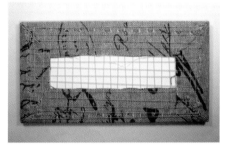

4. Starting with the longest edges, lace together the back of the embroidery, following the instructions in Chapter 2.

5. The back of the lid is then covered using a panel of interlining cut 6mm smaller on the height and width measurements and then covered using tape in the same way as the card. The panel is then ladder stitched into place making sure that there is an even gap of 2–3mm around all edges.

6. The lid can then be attached to the box using buttonhole thread for extra strength with a ladder holding stitch to start and finish the thread.

CHAPTER 5

BOXES WITH OPEN SIDES – ETUI BOXES

oxes with open sides, also known as etui boxes, are traditionally used for storing sewing equipment such as scissors, needles, thimbles and tape measures. The advantage of constructing a box that has collapsible sides is that it can open out fully and either lie flat on the desk or, if godets – triangular panels of fabric – have been added to the sides, the box becomes a tray when opened to stop items that roll from falling out. They can also be useful if you are working on a project that uses beads or even for goldwork, as the sides can be folded up when you have a break, keeping your materials safe. The interior of the base could be covered with velvet, like the boards used to keep the gold chippings or beads in place while you work.

An overlap lid must be used for this style of box, because it is this that holds all the sides together. Etui boxes can be made in any shape except a circle; boxes with multiple sides allow for more items to be stored separately, which is useful if you have a lot of tools. The lid can either

Close-up of the canvas stitches on the etui box.

be constructed first, especially if you are using canvas embroidery that is a set size, or it can be constructed after the rest of the box has been completed. If the box will have more than four sides and will have godets added then I would recommend constructing the lid after the box because it is sometimes difficult to predict what effect the extra fabric will have on the final size of the box.

The sides will usually have a piece of ribbon or ric-rac secured between the interior and exterior pieces to hold the items you wish to store within the box. There is also the option to add a smaller box in the centre of the base for a thimble or pin cushion (in a larger box). The small box could be surrounded by smaller panels, which are the same height, or slightly smaller than the exterior panels for thinner items (stilettos, for example), and positioned so that they fall between two larger exterior panels. The interior sides of the box and the lid for an etui box are best if soft mounted (without card) around interlining to the exterior panels; this is so that you can use the padded interior sections to hold needles and pins as well as ensuring a better fit once the sides are closed.

Hints and tips

Fusible interlining will hold the canvas sides in place, after soft mounting, without causing the wrinkles or distorting that stitches might produce. Using an interlining patch still allows a bit of stretch when it is attached to the interior lid panel.

If you are using canvas as the embroidery for your lid then you will also have to make or buy a cord to sew around the edge of the lid to cover the edges of the canvas, especially if the edges are slightly uneven from the soft mounting process. I think it is nicer if you can use the threads from the embroidery to make a cord that matches and is the correct size for the box, but if this is not possible you should be able to find one to match in most good haberdashery departments. If you are not using canvas your embroidery can be mitred and laced over card following the instructions in Chapter 2.

It is possible to buy a cord maker but if you make cord only occasionally then there are various ways to do it by hand. This cord uses three colours of perlé thread from the design; each colour was made up of four strands of perlé, twisted together to create the cord. Further instructions for hand winding can be found in Chapter 2.

ETUI SEWING BOX

You will need

- Conservation board
- Patchwork cotton for the exterior
- Plain cotton in a contrasting colour for the interior
- Embroidered canvas
- Heavyweight fusible interlining
- Sewing thread
- Buttonhole thread
- Narrow double-sided tape
- Propelling pencil
- Metal ruler
- Set square
- Stanley knife
- Rotary cutter
- Cutting mat
- Embroidery scissors
- Fine curved needle
- Pins
- Cord to match the colours of the box
- White felt

CONSTRUCTING THE OVERLAP LID

Usually you would start by constructing the box first but because the embroidery for this box is canvas and therefore in this case worked to a set size, the lid is constructed first to ensure that the embroidery fits perfectly within the top section of the lid. If you are making an overlap lid not using canvas, the interior sections of the lid would all be constructed first using card and then the exterior would be constructed after checking sizes, similar to making a box base but shallower. There is no set depth for the sides of the lid – it really depends on how big the box is and the style you are aiming for; as this lid holds together the sides of the box I recommend a deeper lid of 2.5cm.

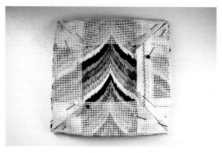

1. Because the canvas is thick enough and strong enough to hold its shape it is not going to be stretched over card. Start by mitring the corners (see Chapter 2 for instructions) so that the canvas is soft mounted.

2. Trim any excess canvas and pin the sides so they stay in place. Cut a small square of the fusible interlining using a metal ruler and rotary cutter, large enough to just cover the cut edges of the canvas, and iron into place.

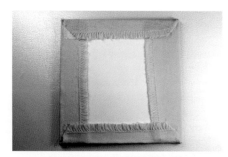

3. Cut and cover with the interior fabric a panel of card to match the size of the now soft mounted canvas embroidery.

4. The canvas can now be attached to the interior panel with wrong sides together using buttonhole thread to ladder stitch on all edges.

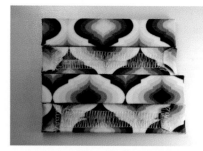

5. After checking the length of the sides, cut and cover two side panels of card the same length as the lid top panel and two 6mm longer than the first two side panels so that they will overlap them when joined.

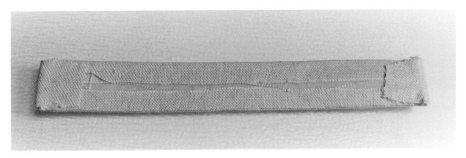

6. Measure the thickness of the embroidered top panel and deduct this measurement from the depth of the sides to give you the depth of the interior panels. Cut out four lengths of interlining all the same length as the two smaller covered card sides (using a metal ruler and a rotary cutter).

7. Iron the interlining panels following the grain straight onto the interior fabric making and leaving enough of an allowance between them for them to be covered in the same way as card, attaching both long sides to one length of tape to avoid adding extra thickness.

8. The covered interlining panels can then be joined onto the side panels so that the bottom edges are level, and ladder stitched into place. Make sure that the two longer pieces have an equally spaced gap at each end for the shorter side pieces to sit in when joined.

9. Placing one long panel against one short panel so that the short panel sits flush with the end of the long side, sew together using ladder stitch.

10. Attach the remaining long side panel to the other end of the first short side panel using ladder stitch.

Hints and tips

• If your canvas embroidery is larger than 10cm², has taken a long time to embroider and is not square, then it is recommended that you stretch the canvas by wetting it (providing you have checked for colour fastness) and stretching it on a wooden board using nails to secure it in place, with the finished size and shape drawn underneath a clear plastic sheet to act as a guide.

• The project's interior panels in the lid are constructed using interlining, which can be cut to the same measurement for all pieces – because it is so thin you don't need to allow for an overlap. If you are using card on the inside then you would want to cut two sides shorter than the others to allow one end to cross over the other, therefore allowing for the thickness of the card, just as with making the exterior pieces of the lid.

11. Then secure the remaining short side panel to the end of the previous long side so that they are all joined in a continuous length.

12. The continuous length of side pieces now needs to be joined to the embroidered top. Start by lining up the interior of the unjoined long side with the interior side of the embroidered top; ladder stitch along the interior join, making sure that if there is a top and bottom to your embroidery design that the longer sides are on the top and bottom edges.

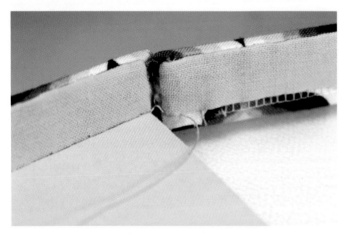

13. Continue to join all the other panels in the joined length to the lid top, stitching the first stitch of each new panel before pressing it against the embroidered top to continue securing the sides together.

14. Once all side panels are secured then the last corner of the sides can be joined together using ladder stitch.

If you have used canvas for your embroidery, to ensure that none of the raw edges or interior fabric is visible a matching cord is attached along the edges, as there is likely to be a small gap between the embroidered top and the sides. It is possible to buy readymade cord or you can make one. This cord is made using four lengths of the three different coloured threads from the embroidery, wound into a 3-ply cord (see instructions in Chapter 2).

1. Ladder stitch is used to sew on the matching cord between the sides and embroidery; the needle is passed through the cord so that it is held by the 'ladder step' between the hidden stitches. To make sure the sewing thread is hidden, it is important to only stitch through the bottom third of the cord while twisting the cord to maintain the correct twist tension throughout. Start attaching the cord slightly in from a corner, leaving a tail of 3–4cm.

2. When you reach the first corner the cord should be twisted slightly more than on the straight parts so that the correct twist pattern is maintained. Even if you have to shorten or lengthen the spacing of the stitches slightly, it is best to bring the needle out at the corner of the embroidery and pass through the cord before stitching on to the side.

3. When you are nearly back at the beginning, the cord will need to be secured, again leaving a short tail of 3–4cm. The cord is secured by sewing through and around it with an embroidery needle and sewing thread, maintaining the twist tension as much as possible.

4. The tail at the beginning of the cord also needs to be secured using the same method but it is divided into separate colours so that the cord sections can be manipulated individually and the main securing thread removed. A bulldog clip is used temporarily to stop them untwisting.

5. The end of the cord can then be secured to the interior top section so that the end sits below the rest of the cord.

6. The beginning threads of the cord can then be secured one at a time (still using ladder stitch) by using a mellor to push them below the end section of cord maintaining the twist pattern so that you have a near-seamless join.

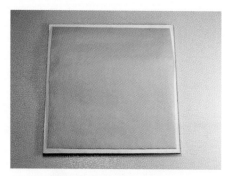

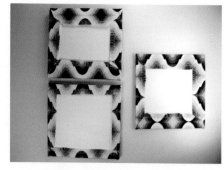

1. Measure the interior measurements of the lid. Using these measurements cut a base for the box which is 2mm smaller on each side than the interior lid measurements. Then cut out a piece of interlining 2mm smaller than the base on all sides.

2. Cut two side panels the same width as the base panel by the required height of the box and two smaller side panels, 6mm narrower than the first two side panels but the same height. Cover the base and side panels with the exterior fabric.

3. Cut out interlining for all four sides, the same size as the smaller side panels minus 2mm from the height. Iron all of the interlining pieces onto a piece of white felt and cut around the interlining so that the joined pieces become the interior panels.

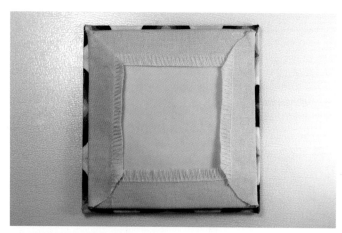

4. Cover all interior felt/interlining panels with the interior fabric. This can be done with double-sided tape as you would do card.

5. Place the base covered interlining panel onto the base; secure on all sides with ladder stitch making sure that there is a 2mm gap on all sides.

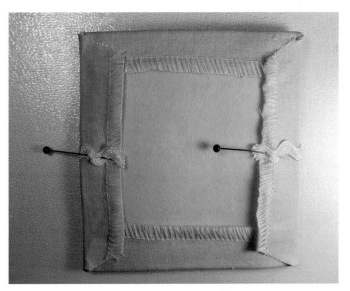

6. Pin the ric-rac to the centre of each side at the back of the remaining interlining side panels.

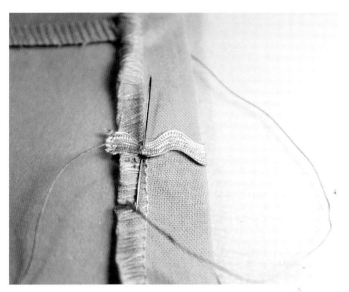

7. Using an embroidery needle, sew each side of the ric-rac onto the covered interlining side panel working from each side to the middle rather than over-sewing; repeat this on all side panels.

8. The interior interlined panels can then be joined onto the exterior side panels, ladder stitching around all edges. There should be a 2mm gap at the bottom of all four panels and a 2mm gap on each side of the wider side panels.

9. The side panels can then be joined one at a time only along the bottom edge to the base with ladder stitch; use a ladder holding stitch at the start and end of each panel. Take care to place each set of matching sides opposite each other.

CHAPTER 6

SHAPED BOXES

Boxes can be made in a wide variety of shapes; they can have more than four sides or only one. There are some limitations due to the card and fabrics but you should generally be able to create a box in most shapes. Triangles are perhaps the hardest shape to create, the angle of the triangle important to bear in mind in terms of being able to cover the points effectively without leaving too small an allowance at the back of the card; equilateral triangles would be best rather than those with sharp points.

Lids of any style can be used on most shaped boxes with the exception of those needing hinges which cannot be used for circular boxes. Lift-out lids work particularly well for shaped boxes that could also be made up of several shaped boxes joined together, in a honeycomb pattern for instance. This allows the boxes to sit side by side without having the overlapping sides of a box lid preventing the sides from meeting. If you wished to have an overlapping lid with a bit of planning I'm sure it would be possible to join together several lids with only the exterior edges having side panels.

Depending on the style of lid any fabric and embroidery style can be used for shaped boxes. The embroidery design would ideally need to be planned around the shape of the box you wish to make. If you have a design already completed that would work well on a particular shape the box and lid could be designed around the completed embroidery. Thicker fabrics will need to be taken into account when working out the sizes of panels for the boxes.

The construction method used for the pentagon box project would be the same for a hexagon, triangle and other multiple-sided boxes; the sides should have a staggered overlap so that the thin end of the panels is used as part of the length of the side you are creating. Other construction methods would suggest the sides are laid out along a continuous length of fabric and laced together so that there is only one seam. I prefer to create each side panel separately; this obviously takes more time but you have more control over separate panels than a long length of shifting panels. In my opinion having separate sides gives a neater and stronger finish as the sides are joined separately and not just relying on the tightness of the fabric to hold them in the correct position. This also means that if any of the panels are slightly the wrong size to fit to the base shape, one panel can easily be adjusted without having to remove all of the other panels as well.

Pentagonal and circular boxes.

··❧[PROJECT]❧··

PENTAGON-SHAPED MEMORY BOX WITH LIFT-OUT LID

You will need

- Conservation board
- Crushed shimmer polyester for the exterior
- Quilting cotton for the interior
- Lightweight calico
- Cotton bump
- Sewing and buttonhole thread
- Ribbon for lid pull
- Narrow double-sided tape
- Glue
- Acid-free tissue paper
- Propelling pencil
- Metal ruler
- Set square
- Stanley knife
- Cutting mat
- Embroidery and fabric scissors
- Fine curved needle
- Pins

Pentagon shaped box with goldwork embroidery.

CONSTRUCTING THE INTERIOR

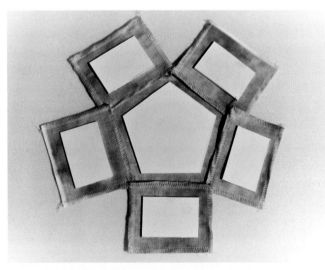

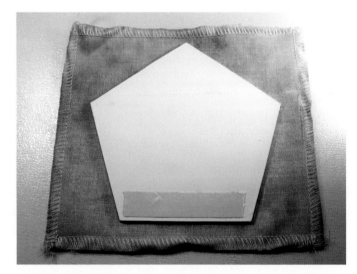

1. Using a pentagon template, draw around the shape with a propelling pencil onto the conservation card and then neaten with a ruler. Repeat two more times and cut out the interior base and two lid panels for the box, putting the lids to one side. Measure the length of the pentagon's sides and cut out five side panels 3mm narrower than the length of the pentagon's sides by the desired height of the internal box. Cut out a piece of interior fabric for the base and side panels 2cm bigger than the panels on each side.

2. Cover the side panels and the base panel of the box with the interior fabric. To cover the pentagon, start by taping and folding over the fabric on the bottom edge.

3. Then fold the fabric over the top two edges either side of the point, making sure to place the fabric under a small amount of tension. The remaining two sides can then be secured with a small amount of tension so the fabric is taut.

4. Holding two of the side panels together, so that one of the side panels is flush with the end of the other, join them together using ladder stitch with the right side facing inwards.

5. The joined panels are then attached to the base. The joined thin exterior edge of the first panel should line up with the corner point leaving a gap at the opposite end for a panel to be added later. The second panel is flush with the next edge of the base; the unjoined exterior edge will line up with the next base corner point so that all sides will be overlapping once completed.

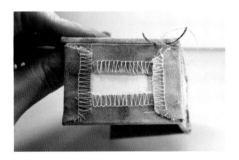

6. Attach the third panel by placing it in the gap at the end of the first side panel. Using ladder stitch, starting by joining it to the top of the first panel and then down onto the base; again there will be a gap at the end of the side before the corner for the next side.

7. Join the fourth panel by placing it in the gap at the end of the third panel. This should be done in the same way as the third side.

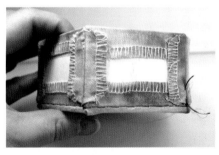

8. Attach the fifth panel by placing it in the gap at the end of the fourth panel. This should be done in the same way as the fourth panel but continuing the ladder stitch to close the final join between the fifth and second panel.

1. Taking one of the lid panels of card, use it as a template to cut a pentagon of cotton bump; put the bump to one side as it will sit between the calico-covered card and the goldwork embroidery.

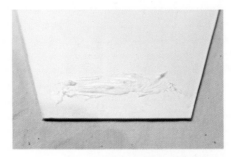

2. Using a small paintbrush and craft glue, cover the lid with the lightweight calico, folding in the same order used to cover the interior base panel. Make sure that you leave a gap of 1–1.5cm between the glue and the edge of the card.

3. Trim the calico back at an angle, in the same way you would if using tape, to just before each point, so that when the allowance is folded over there are only two layers of calico overlapping. Leave for the glue to dry completely.

4. Place the previously cut pentagon of cotton bump on top of the right side of the calico-covered panel.

5. Place the embroidered fabric over the top of the cotton bump and, using the tacked pentagon outline already on the embroidery to place it in the correct position, pin the bottom edge to the card.

6. Pulling the fabric at a slight tension, pin the two sides opposite the bottom into place.

7. The remaining two sides are then pulled at a tension and pinned into place. If the tacking line is not the same distance from the edge of the card on all sides, adjust the pins and pull or relax the fabric until the lines are the same all the way around.

8. Mounting goldwork embroideries, whether for a box or for a frame, will require a supporting frame made out of rolled up acid-free tissue paper in order to stop the goldwork from cracking or being squashed during the mounting process.

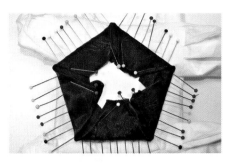

9. Lacing requires an even number of sides so that opposite sides can be laced together. As a pentagon has five sides this piece will need to be mounted using the traditional form of mounting, starting by pinning the points into a mitre (see Chapter 2 for full instructions).

11. A herringbone stitch should then be used to secure the edges of the embroidery to the calico underneath, following the instructions from Chapter 2. The herringbone should be worked around all edges of the pentagon using a dark-coloured buttonhole thread.

13. Cut a piece of ribbon 5–6cm long and pin to the back of the lid panel on the bottom edge, creating a loop. Secure in place, working the stitches from the edge to the middle of the ribbon.

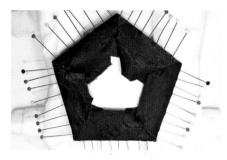

10. As you will see from the traditional mounting instructions in Chapter 2, mitred corners are usually stitched together as the herringbone stitch (to secure the sides) reaches each corner. If you have made a larger pentagon box I would also do this but as this pentagon is small it is best to stitch the mitred corners into place first. There isn't enough room to pull the fabric between them at a tight enough tension with all the pins in the way.

12. The tacking stitches can then be removed from the edge of the lid using a mellor to prevent damage to the material.

14. The interior panel of the lid can then be covered with the interior fabric. Making sure that the edges are lined up perfectly, join the interior lid to the embroidered lid with ladder stitch, making sure that the needle passes through the middle of the ribbon to hold it in the correct position.

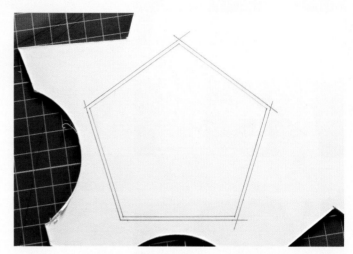

1. Measure the finished height of the interior box and lid. The lid will sit within the height of the exterior side panels so it is important to make sure the side panels are high enough. This measurement will be needed for the height of the exterior sides.

2. Draw around the pentagon template used for the base and lid panels and then increase the size by 3mm for the exterior base. Do not cut out until the exterior sides have been constructed. Measure the length of the extended sides and use this measurement minus 3mm to cut out five sides using the height measurement from the total interior and lid height.

3. The sides are then covered with the exterior fabric; the top corners need to be mitred because they will be visible above the interior sides (mitre instructions in Chapter 2). The bottom edge can be secured with tape as usual. Fold in the top corners to form the mitre, pin in place, then use tape to secure the main length of the fabric at the top before sewing up the mitred corners and then folding in bottom corners so the sides are secured onto tape.

4. Holding two of the sides together, so that the side on the left is flush with the end of the side on the right, join them together using ladder stitch with the right side facing outwards and the mitred corners at the top.

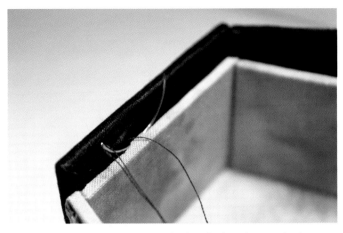

5. The joined sides are then attached to the interior panels along the top edge of the interior using ladder stitch. The end of the first exterior panel should line up with the end of an interior panel so that the second panel wraps around following the same staggered joins as the interior panels. Take care when carrying the thread over to the second panel.

6. Attach the third panel by placing it at the end of the second side. Using ladder stitch, continue the previous thread from the second panel to join the third panel to the interior panel.

7. Starting a new thread, ladder stitch the exterior join between the two sides together.

8. Repeat steps 6 and 7 until all five sides have been joined to the interior.

9. Check the measurements for the base and make any necessary adjustments. Then cut the base out and cover with the exterior fabric in the same way as the interior base and lid sections. Place the covered base on to the bottom of the box and secure in place using ladder stitch and ladder holding stitch.

··❧[PROJECT]❧··

ROUND BRACELET BOX WITH FITTED LID

You will need

- Conservation board
- Thin mountboard (1mm or less)
- Silk for the exterior
- Quilting cotton for the interior
- Felt similar in colour to the exterior fabric
- Lightweight calico
- Sewing and buttonhole thread
- Narrow double-sided tape
- Propelling pencil
- Fabric pencil
- Metal ruler
- Set square
- Stanley knife
- Compass circle cutter
- Cutting mat
- Embroidery and fabric scissors
- Fine curved needle
- Pins
- Crystal beads

Bracelet box with stumpwork flowers.

CONSTRUCTING THE INTERIOR LID AND BASE

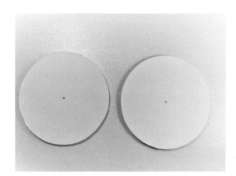

1. Measure the widest part of the object that you wish to store in the box, in this case a bracelet, and add 1.5–2cm; this will be the diameter of the internal box. Use this measurement to cut out two circles using a compass circle cutter following the tip in Chapter 2.

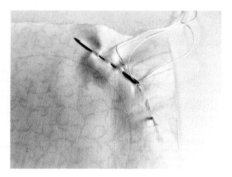

2. Draw around the circles on the wrong side of the interior fabric with a fabric pencil and then work a running stitch, using a long length of buttonhole thread, 1cm away from the pencil line all the way around.

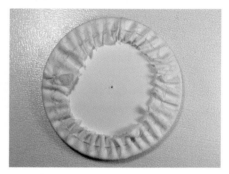

3. Place one of the card circles in the centre of the fabric and pull the thread tightly to gather the fabric around the card. Secure the thread into place.

4. The back of the circle then needs to be laced to pull the fabric to the correct tension. This can be done by stitching from one side to the other but crossing over the previous stitch so that the lacing is worked in a circle and the stitches remain parallel to each other. Repeat steps 2–4 to cover the remaining circle of card with the interior fabric.

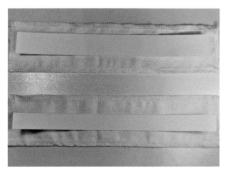

5. Measure the circumference of the circle using a flexible tape measure; take 2mm off this measurement to give you the length of the sides. The side panels can then be cut from the thinner mount card. The sides should be cut with different heights: a bigger height for the lid and a smaller height for the base.

6. The side panels are then covered with the interior fabric. The top corners of the lid side need to be mitred because they will be visible below the exterior sides (mitre instructions are given in Chapter 2). This can be done using tape to secure the main length of the fabric and then folding in the corners before sewing up the mitred corner. The bottom edge can be secured with tape as usual.

7. The side panels are then ladder stitched to the interior circle bases. Leaving the ends unjoined, place the base on top of a tape measure or other item to give you enough height for the side and work around the edge of the base until the two ends meet. The mitred corners for the lid should be at the top of the side and facing outwards.

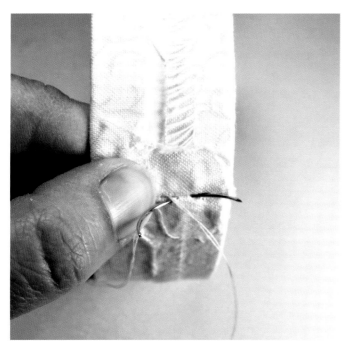

9. The two interior sections can then be placed together to check that they fit correctly.

8. The two ends are then joined by continuing the thread up from the base. Repeat steps 7 and 8 with the other base and side.

1. Measure the diameter of the circles with the added sides and cut out two more circles for the exterior lid and base. Check that the circles fit well on top of the interior sections of the box and make any adjustments.

2. Cover one of the circles with felt of a similar colour to the silk exterior fabric.

3. Draw around the felt covered circle on the wrong side of the exterior fabric with a fabric pencil.

4. A tacking line in a contrasting coloured thread is then stitched along the pencil line but not pulled tight. The fabric is then placed in a ring frame along with lightweight calico behind it.

5. The stumpwork petals that have been worked specifically for this box (see stitch plan in Chapter 8) are then positioned within the circle with five petals used to create a single flower. Each of the petals is curled around a pencil before being stitched into place.

6. Using a stiletto to make a hole for the wire ends, each of the petals' wire ends are then plunged through the hole to the back of the frame.

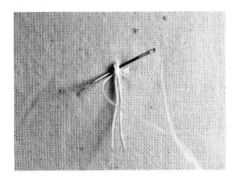

7. The ends of the wire are then secured in place by over-sewing with a double sewing thread, making sure to catch just the calico at the back and not the silk.

8. Repeating steps 6 and 7, create a five-petal flower at the top of the circle, with two more five-petal flowers sitting either side underneath the first.

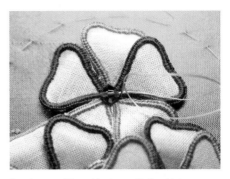

9. A crystal bead is then stitched into the centre of each flower to finish off the centre and cover any gaps between petals.

10. Using the tacking line as a guide pin the embroidered fabric to the edge of the felt-covered circle.

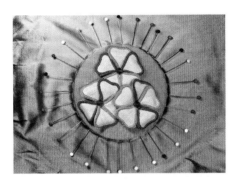

11. Once the fabric has been pinned all the way around the circle, readjust each pin, pulling the fabric slightly so that there is a tight tension across the fabric.

12. Turn the circle over and trim back the calico to the edge of the card so that it doesn't add extra bulk when mounted. Trim the silk so that it is just longer than the pins used to secure it in place.

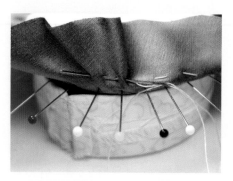

13. Place the lid onto one of the interior parts to protect the flowers and use buttonhole thread to stitch a running stitch around the silk, approximately 1cm away from the tacking line.

14. The buttonhole thread can then be pulled tight to gather the silk around the lid.

15. The back of the circle then needs to be laced to pull the fabric to the correct tension by stitching from one side to the other, as before.

16. The tacking stitches can then be removed from the edge of the lid using a mellor to avoid damaging the fabric.

17. The exterior lid top is then ladder stitched to the interior side panel of the lid (the larger of the two interior sections) using ladder stitch.

18. The base of the box is also covered with the exterior silk in the same way as the interior panels were covered; follow steps 2 to 4 in constructing the interior lid and base section.

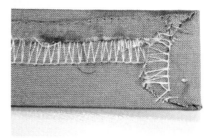

19. The exterior base is then ladder stitched to the interior sides of the base (the smaller of the two interior sections) using ladder stitch.

20. Check the final height measurements of the joined lid and base sections; cut two exterior sides from the thinner mount card adding 2mm to the interior circumference measurement. The height of each piece should be the same, 5mm deeper than the interior base and 5mm smaller than the interior lid.

21. The sides are then covered with the exterior fabric; the top corners of the base side need to be mitred because they will be visible above the interior sides (see instructions in Chapter 2). This can be done using tape to secure the main length of the fabric and then folding in the corners before sewing up the mitred corner. The bottom edge can be secured with tape as usual.

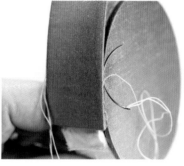

22. The top of the un-mitred lid side is then ladder stitched to the exterior top. Leaving the ends unjoined, place the side on top of the interior join and work around the edge of the exterior top until the two ends meet.

23. The two ends are then joined by continuing the thread up from the base; then continue around the bottom edge of the exterior side.

24. For the base section this step and step 25 must be worked at the same time, alternating between the two edges. The mitred exterior side is then ladder stitched to the exterior base, making sure that the mitred corners are above the top edge of the interior section. Leaving the ends unjoined, place the side on top of the interior join and ladder stitch along the bottom edge to join the side to the exterior base.

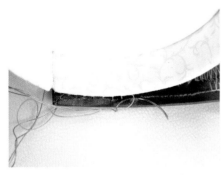

25. At the same time as the bottom edge is joined to the base; the exterior base side is also ladder stitched along the inside to the top edge of the interior side.

26. The two ends are then joined by continuing the thread up from the base.

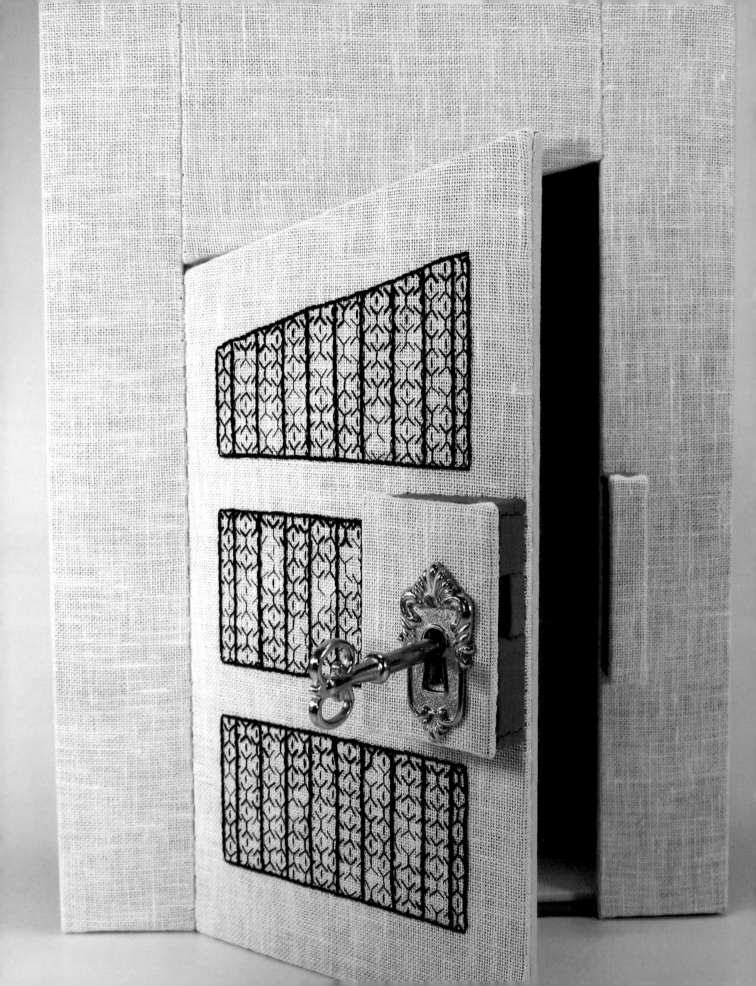

ADVANCED CONSTRUCTION

Once you have mastered the construction methods set out in the previous chapters you can start to add more complex construction elements to your box designs, such as mirrors, false bottoms and working locks. False bottoms and mirrors are the least complex of the advanced elements that you could add to your box, so I would suggest starting with these two first and then working towards adding a lock.

False bottoms can be added to any shape and size of box as long as the correct support system is in place. False bottoms are designed to fit as closely to the sides of the box as possible in order to hide extra space below. Therefore extra supports need to be included in the construction of the main box, similar to those for a tray; these supports also need to have one end cut at an angle in order to be able to push down and tilt the bottom when you wish to remove it. On a square or rectangular box you will only need two supports but on a box with multiple sides

you may need more than two – it really depends on the shape and size of the box and how the false bottom will be removed from the box. Tags can be attached to the false bottom to help with removal from the bottom of the box if you are using two layers of card but in some cases you may wish to use only a single covered layer.

Mirrors ideally need to have extra space to fit within the lid of a box, and the chest lid is perfect for this. It is also possible to mount them within an overlap or fitted lid; you would need an extra frame of card to surround the mirror layer so that the lid is flat rather than curved over the mirror (the extra layer of card can be hidden by the side panels). Cutting and covering the hole for the mirror can be a bit fiddly but it is worth the effort. The corners of the interior frame are covered with small strips of fabric prior to the main cover. It is therefore important to choose a fabric with a small amount of give but one that does not fray easily once glued. An alternative method, which would work best with a larger mirror, would be to create the frame surround using four panels joined together. This would be the best method

if you wished to embroider a design for around the frame of the mirror; it is not advisable to have embroidery with the other method because it would not be possible to lace to the correct tension.

Locks can be a particularly impressive addition to any box, especially if they are functioning locks rather than just for aesthetics. There are several types of locks that can be used for a box; the one you use will depend on the style of box you are constructing. For cupboard doors like the project in this chapter you make a casing for the lock to sit in and a keep for the locking mechanism to secure to. If you were to fit the lock to an internal lid you would need to create a deeper lid with a hollow centre between two pieces of card, with side panels all the way around. The hollow centre around the lock can then be padded out, either with pillars made out of blocks of card taped together or pillars of several sticky foam pads. If the lock is to be fitted into a fitted lid then the interior front panels of both the box and the lid need to be padded out in a similar way to create a space for the lock while still providing support across the whole panel.

Close-up of a locking door on
the wedding card box.

··⁊[PROJECT]⁊··

TRAVEL JEWELLERY BOX WITH MIRROR AND FALSE BOTTOM

You will need

- Conservation board
- Thin mountboard
- Silk dupion for the exterior
- Contrasting silk dupion for the interior
- Small mirror
- Sewing and buttonhole thread
- Narrow double-sided tape
- Glue
- Paintbrush

- Propelling pencil
- Metal ruler
- Set square
- Stanley knife
- Cutting mat
- Embroidery and fabric scissors
- Fine curved needle
- Pins

Chest box with smocking embroidery, mirror and false bottom.

CONSTRUCTING THE INTERIOR BOX WITH FALSE BOTTOM SUPPORTS

1. Decide on the internal measurements of the box base and cut two long sides and two short sides, taking 6mm off the width of the short sides for the thickness of the longer sides. The sides will all be the same height measurement and then all four sides need to be covered in the interior silk fabric.

2. Placing a short side so that it sits against the inside edge of a long side, attach the small side to the long side.

4. Cut and cover the supports for the false bottom. Each support should be cut as a rectangle 6mm shorter than the length of the long side and depending on the required height of the false-bottomed section only 1–2cm in height. One end of each support should then be cut at an approximately 45° angle. Make sure that the sides are covered so that the right side of one is on the opposite side to the other.

3. The second short side is then joined to the other end of the long side.

6. The first support can then be ladder stitched to the long side working from the bottom edge and then around all the support edges.

7. The second long side can then be joined to one of the smaller sides so that the smaller side sits against the inside edge of a long side.

5. Place one of the supports along the bottom of the joined long side so that there is a gap at each end. Make sure that the two smaller sides can be lifted up into their finished position and that the straight end of the support is flush with the small side next to it.

8. Place the second false bottom support against the bottom edge of the second long side (the point of the support should be in the opposite direction to the first), and secure in place in the same way.

9. Join the final corner of the box together with the short side placed so that it sits against the inside edge of the second long side.

10. Measure the final dimensions of the interior box sides and cut a base to fit flush with the exterior edges of the interior sides and cover with the interior fabric.

11. Attach the interior base to the constructed interior sides on all edges.

1. Measure the height, length and width of the completed interior sides of the box. Cut out and cover four exterior sides all with the same height as the constructed interior box, minus 1mm for fabric thickness. The smaller sides are the same width as the smaller side of the constructed box (including the thickness of the long sides), minus 1mm for fabric thickness. The long sides are the same length as the constructed interior long side plus 6mm for the thickness of the smaller sides that they will overlap.

2. Placing a short side so that it sits against the inside edge of a long side, attach the small side to the long side. The second short side is then joined to the other end of the long side.

3. The second long side can then be joined to one of the smaller sides so that the smaller side sits against the inside edge of a long side. Then the joined sides are wrapped around the constructed interior.

4. Join the final corner of the box together with the short side placed so that it sits against the inside edge of the second long side. Work the thread from the bottom of one side to the top edges and then continue to stitch between the interior and exterior tops, all the way around the box, to join them together.

5. Measure the final dimensions of the exterior box and cut a base to fit flush with the exterior edges and cover with the exterior fabric. Attach the exterior base to the constructed exterior sides on all edges.

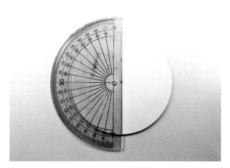

1. Measure the width of the box and, using this measurement minus 4mm as the diameter, cut out a circle using a compass circle cutter following the tip in Chapter 2. The circle is then cut in half to become the two ends of the chest lid. Use a protractor as a guide to make sure it is divided equally.

2. One of the semicircle ends is then covered by lacing the exterior fabric into place (following instructions in Chapter 2) rather than taped because it produces a better finish on a curved edge. Start to work from top to bottom across the width of the semicircle.

3. Then work the ladder stitch from side to side starting from the curve to the straight edge, folding in the ends of the fabric so that a neat uncreased edge is created.

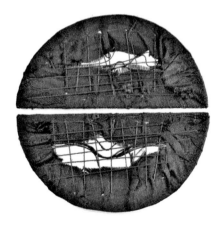

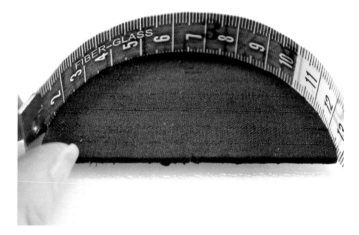

4. Steps 2 and 3 are repeated to cover the other semicircle. It doesn't matter if they are bulky due to folds in the fabric because they will be hidden behind the mirror section later.

5. Measure the curve of the semicircles using a flexible tape measure; this will give you the depth of the exterior lid. The length measurement used for the long exterior sides of the constructed box is also used for the length of the exterior lid. Cut out a thin panel of mountboard using these two measurements and check that the depth sides are the correct length by curving it around the edge of the semicircle it will be joined to.

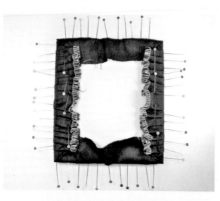

6. Place the Canadian smocked embroidery onto the exterior lid top and pin in place starting with the longer sides, making sure that the smocking is centred across the lid. The shorter sides which have folds created by the smocking are folded into neat and evenly spaced pleats and pinned into place. The pleats are folded starting at each end and working to the middle; the pleats change direction in the middle to give a neater finish and follow the natural folds formed by the smocking.

7. The corners are then mitred following the instructions in Chapter 2 before the pleats are then continued round to the back of the lid and pinned into place ready for lacing.

8. The lid top then needs to be laced, Start by working the stitches from one pleated side to the other to hold them securely in place, removing only the pins securing the pleats as you go.

9. The other sides are then laced into place. Leave the end of the thread unsecured as the thread will be pulled tight after the sides have been attached to the top.

10. Stitch the semicircles to each pleated edge of the lid top so that the unpleated edges are flush with the bottom straight edge of the semicircle.

11. Measure the finished depth of the ends and then pull the unsecured thread from the lacing until the unpleated edges are the same depth all the way along. Secure the thread.

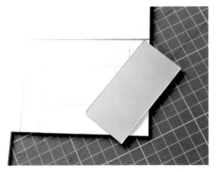

1. Measure the internal space of the constructed exterior of the lid and using those measurements minus 1mm from the width and length, cut a rectangle of board. Measure the mirror to be fitted into the centre of the lid, then mark and cut out a rectangle in the centre of the board that is 5–6mm smaller than the width and length measurements of the mirror.

2. In order to prevent the interior corners of the card from showing once the silk has been cut for the mirror, the corners need to be covered using a spare piece of the interior fabric. Tape is firstly used to secure the small piece of silk on both sides of the shorter side of the internal rectangle.

3. Notches are then cut into the silk, stopping just before the internal corners, and the unsecured fabric is pulled and taped into place adjacent to the first taped edge. This is done on the front and back of the card so that the corners have a continuous length with the fabric cut on the front and back.

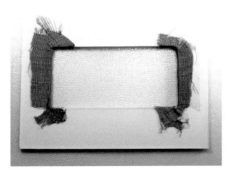

4. Steps 2 and 3 are then repeated on the opposite sets of corners.

5. The interior top is then covered with the interior silk fabric using double-sided tape (following the instructions in Chapter 2).

6. Using a pair of fine pointed scissors a line is cut in the centre of the mirror space along its length leaving an uncut gap of approximately 1cm at each end. A small amount of craft glue is then applied in all four corners and left to dry.

7. Using the same pair of scissors, cut the silk from the line already cut to the glued corners, stopping about 1–2mm from the corner.

8. Sticking lengths of tape to the edges of the internal rectangle, fold the flaps of silk back to cover the edges of the internal rectangle.

9. Place the mirror in the centre of the interior lid and secure two opposite corners into place using a double length of sewing thread. This is done by stitching diagonally across the corner, taking the needle through the fabric approximately 1–1.5cm away from the corner point on each side of the corner. This should be secure enough to hold the mirror in place, but if you are using a larger mirror then you may wish to secure all four corners.

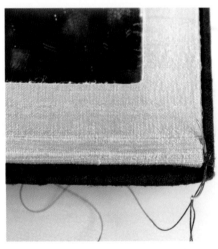

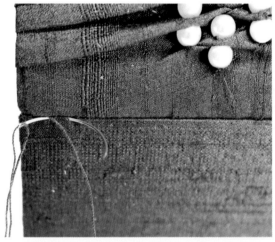

10. Place the interior lid into the exterior lid and, making sure that the interior edges remain flush with the exterior sides, stitch into place on all edges.

11. The finished lid is then placed onto the constructed box and, using the ladder holding stitch to start and finish the thread, stitch the lid to the back edge of the box.

1. Measure the interior space of the box where the false bottom will sit and cut a panel of card 2mm smaller on the width and length.

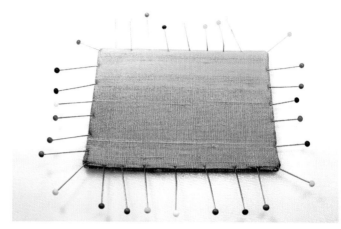

2. Cover the false bottom with the interior fabric, leaving a small gap between the tape and the edge of the card. The back of the false bottom is then covered in the same way as the back of an embroidery in traditional mounting (see Chapter 2). Pin the interior fabric to the back of the false bottom, starting with the two longest sides, folding under all sides so that the fold is approximately 1mm from the edge of the card.

3. The cover panel is then ladder stitched into place all the way around; use the stitches to pull the fabric so that it is in line with the edge of the card and make sure that the needle is taken out at the point of the cover panel to pull it closer to the corner of the card panel.

4. The false bottom can then be placed into the box and checked to make sure that it can be removed by pressing down on the corners where the angled end of the support is.

·❧[PROJECT]❧·

WEDDING CARD LETTER BOX WITH KEY LOCK

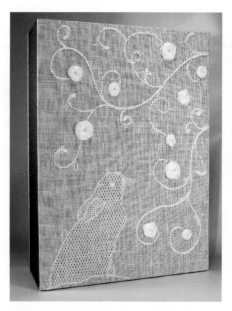

You will need

- Conservation board
- Even-weave linen for the exterior embroidery
- Polycotton for exterior and embroidery backing
- Quilting cotton for the interior
- Small working lock with key
- Sewing and buttonhole thread
- Narrow double-sided tape
- Glue
- Paintbrush
- Propelling pencil
- Metal ruler
- Set square
- Stanley knife
- Cutting mat
- Embroidery and fabric scissors
- Fine curved needle
- Pins

Alice in Wonderland-themed wedding card box with whitework rabbit and ribbonwork white roses.

CONSTRUCTING THE INTERIOR

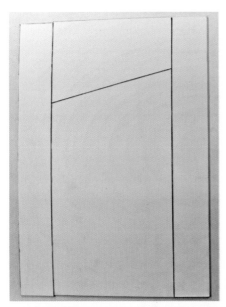

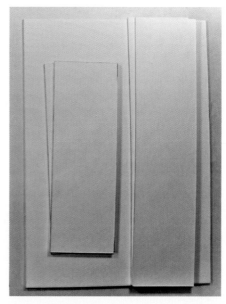

1. Decide on the overall height, width and depth of the box (this box is roughly A4 in size) and taking off 6mm from the width and height measurements cut out a large rectangle for the interior front. This is then divided into three strips by measuring an approximately 3.7cm wide strip in from both of the side edges. The middle strip is then divided into two by measuring down from the top edge 8.5cm along the first vertical line and then 5.4cm on the second line at the top and joining to create an angled top edge for the door. Cut along all lines so that the rectangle is in four panels.

2. Cut out another large rectangle using the same measurements as the front for the interior back. Then cut two sides using the same height measurement as the front and back panels. As the sides will sit between the front and back panels the width of the sides should be the final depth of the box minus 12mm to take off the thickness of the interior and exterior front and back panels. Also cut a top and base; these will not add to the final height of the box so should be cut 6mm smaller than the width of the front/back and the same width as the sides.

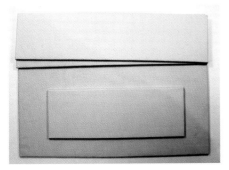

3. Put the front sections to one side for now and cover all of the other interior panels: back, sides, top and base.

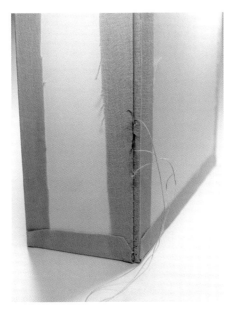

4. Join one of the interior side panels to the interior back; the side panel's edge should sit against the right side of the back panel. The right side of each panel should be facing inwards.

5. Attach the base to the joined side and back panels; the base should sit flush with the width of the side and there should be a small gap left at the other end for the second side to fit into.

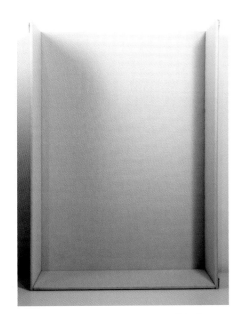

6. Place the remaining side panel in the gap, at the unjoined end of the base, and join the side panel onto the base and back panels.

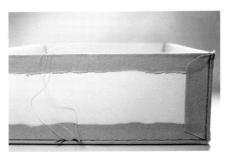

7. Join the top panel along the top edges of the sides and back panels so that it sits flush with all top edges and between the two sides.

8. Take one of the front narrow side strip panels, cover with the interior fabric and join to the partially constructed interior so that three of the exterior edges sit flush against the top, base and side panels.

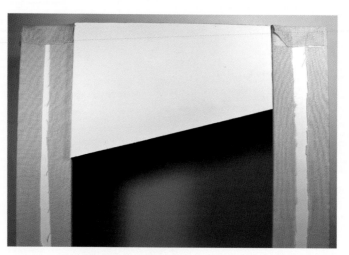

10. Place the uncovered angled top section for the front between the two narrow strips to check how much the thickness of the fabric has affected the fit.

9. Cover the remaining narrow side strip with the interior fabric and join to the opposite side of the partially constructed interior from the first narrow strip, so that it fits against the sides, back and top panels in the same way as the first narrow strip.

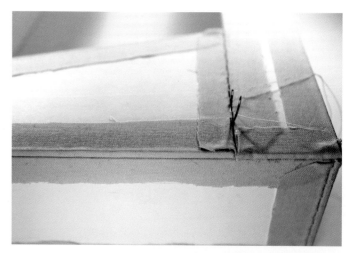

11. Trim the longer edge of the angled front section by between 3 and 4mm depending on the thickness of the interior fabric. Check that it fits with a small gap each side (no more than 1mm) and cover it with the interior fabric; it should now fit perfectly within the two strips.

12. Stitch the angled top front panel into place between the two narrow strips so that it is secured on three edges. The door will be completed last so the interior part of the door is not covered at this point.

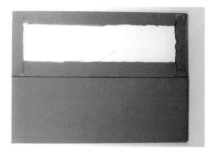

1. Measure the top of the constructed interior panels and cut two panels of board for the exterior top and base to sit flush with all edges of the constructed interior; cover the panels with the exterior fabric.

2. Place the exterior top and base panels so that they are in the correct position on the constructed interior and measure the final height of the box.

3. Using the final height measurement from step 2 and the same width measurement for the top and base panels, cut out two side panels and cover with the exterior fabric.

4. Join the base to one of the side panels so that the right side of the fabric is facing outwards and the base sits against the wrong side of the side panel.

5. Attach the top to the other end of the joined side panel so that like the base, the top sits against the wrong side of the side panel.

6. Join the remaining side panel to the base panel, so that the edge of the base panel sits against the wrong side of the side panel. Wrap the exterior top, base and side panels around the interior sections and join the remaining corner so that the top panel edge sits against the wrong side of the side panel.

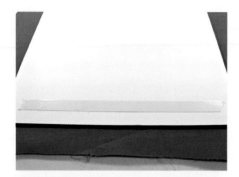

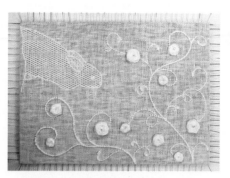

7. Check the width and length measurements for the front and back panels. Using those measurements minus 2mm, cut out two panels of board. Cover the back panel only with the exterior polycotton, placing the tape so that there is an approximately 1cm gap before the edge of the board.

8. Check the measurements of the interior front panels. Using the remaining panel from step 7 divide it into three strips, in the same way as the interior front panels, by measuring an approximately 4cm-wide strip in from both of the side edges. The middle strip is then divided into two by measuring down from the top edge 8.8cm along the first vertical line and then 5.7cm on the second line at the top and joining to create an angled top edge for the door. Cut along all lines so that the rectangle is in four panels. Trim the centre top panel on the longest side by 2mm. Cover the two side strips and top panel for above the door with the exterior polycotton. The door panel is left uncovered to one side with the interior door panel.

9. Place the rabbit and rose embroidery onto the large covered back panel so that the stems for the roses finish on the right-hand edge and the ground beneath the rabbit sits on the bottom edge. Pin to the board so that the grain of the fabric is straight with the edges of the board.

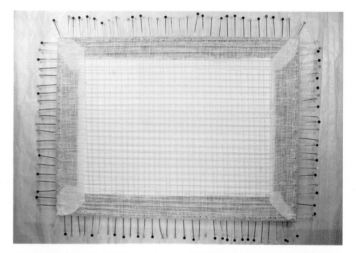

10. Carefully remove the central tacking stitches using a mellor to avoid damaging the fabric or embroidery and trim the linen back to just before the tops of the pins.

11. Placing acid-free tissue paper underneath the board, follow the instructions in Chapter 2 and lace the back of the embroidery, starting by working across the longest sides and then the shortest. Remove the pins and use a mellor to gently smooth out the pinholes.

12. Place the mounted embroidery onto the back of the constructed interior and stitch into place all the way around to the exterior top, base and sides.

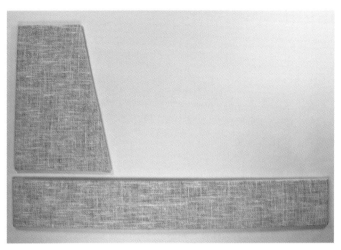

13. Cover both of the side strips and the top panel with the same linen used for the embroideries.

14. Join one of the side strips to the interior side strip, starting at the top and working round the panel up to the bottom of the interior centre top panel above the doorway. The strip should sit flush with the interior edge of the doorway and the exterior edges of the box top, side and base.

15. Join the remaining side strip to the opposite interior side strip in the same way as the first strip in step 14.

16. Place the centre top panel between the two side strips. The top and bottom edges should sit flush with the top of the box and the interior edge of the doorway. Secure in place by stitching around all edges to join to the interior centre top and exterior top and side panels.

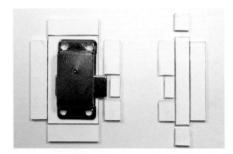

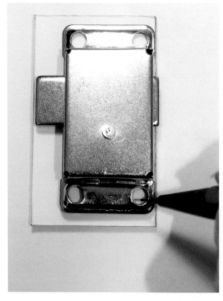

1. Measure the width, length and depth of the lock plate and the deadbolt. Cut a rectangle of board for the top part of the lock casing that is 6mm longer than the lock and 6mm wider than the deadbolt when the lock is in the unlocked position. Cut two side panels the same width as the top by the depth of the lock plate, and a back panel 6mm smaller than the length of the top using the same depth measurement as the sides. The front is divided into three panels so that a gap is created for the deadbolt to slot through. The top panel should be the length between the top of the lock plate and the deadbolt minus 1mm by the depth of the sides and back. The middle panel should be the width of the deadbolt by the depth between the top of the deadbolt and the top of the lock plate. The bottom panel should be the length between the bottom of the deadbolt and the bottom of the lock plate minus 1mm by the depth of the sides and back.

   The top of the lock keep is cut out using the same length measurements as the lock top but only 1cm wide (or wide enough for the deadbolt lock to fit). The back panel is the same size as the back panel for the lock casing. The three front panels should also be cut to the same measurements as the panels from the lock casing. The sides are cut to the same depth as the back panel by the width of the top.

2. The top panel needs a hole cut for the key to pass through. Place the lock into position on the top panel and draw around the corner holes in the lock plate.

3. Place the keyhole cover so that it is centred between the two bottom circle marks and draw around the keyhole. Using the keyhole as a guide, mark a rectangle around it to cut out a straight and even keyhole in the board.

4. Cut out the keyhole from the board and cover with the exterior polycotton. Place small pieces of tape along the inside edges of the keyhole and fold them against the back. Using a fine paintbrush, paint craft glue over all the fabric within the hole and leave to dry.

5. When the glue is dry the fabric can be cut up to each corner to form flaps that are folded back to stick to the tape.

6. Cover the remaining lock casing and keep panels with the exterior polycotton fabric.

7. The lock casing is constructed first: join the back panel to one of the side panels so that the end of the back panel is placed against the wrong side of the side panel with the right sides facing outwards.

8. Join the remaining side panel onto the other end of the back panel in the same way as the first.

9. Join the three front panels together, so that the smallest panel is in the middle of the two larger panels, using small ladder stitches.

10. The joined front panels are then attached to the joined side and back panels so that they sit between the two side panels. Check that the lock fits correctly by placing it within the constructed casing.

11. The keep is then constructed by joining one of the small side panels to the back panel so that the end of the back panel is placed against the wrong side of the side panel with the right sides facing outwards.

12. Join the other side panel onto the opposite end of the back panel in the same way as the first.

13. Join the three front panels together using small ladder stitches, see step 9. The joined front panels are then attached to the joined side and back section so that they sit between the two side panels.

14. Check that the lock casing and lock keep will work correctly with the lock mechanism when it is in the locked position so that the door will lock once they are secured to the door and box.

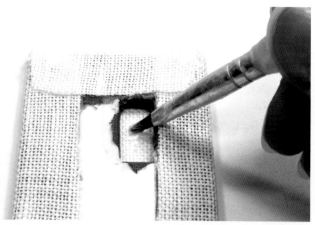

15. The top of the lock casing is then covered in the same linen as the embroidery. Using a fine paintbrush, paint craft glue over all the fabric within the hole and leave to dry.

16. When the glue is dry place small pieces of tape along the inside edges of the keyhole and fold them against the back. The linen can be cut up to each corner to form flaps, which are folded back to stick to the tape.

17. The keyhole cover is then stitched into place over the hole using a double length of sewing thread, which can be secured beneath the cover. Stitch two stitches over the edge of the plate from the hole and into the linen fabric on both ends.

18. Lining up the lock with the keyhole, secure the lock to the wrong side of the top panel by oversewing the corners several times to the linen beneath the lock, using buttonhole thread for strength.

19. Place the top onto the constructed base panels. Starting from the edge of the gap for the deadbolt, stitch the top onto the base panels working all the way around to the other side of the deadbolt gap.

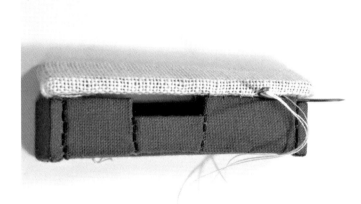

20. Cover the top for the keep with the linen from the embroidery and place on top of the constructed keep base. Stitch into place working all around the top panel.

21. Now that both sections are constructed check that the lock and key work as they should with the casing and keep in the correct positions.

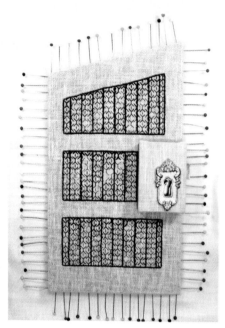

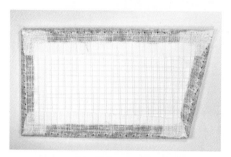

1. Take the two door panels cut from the front panel and check that they are flush with each other at the sides and make any necessary adjustments. The interior door panel should be 3mm shorter than the exterior panel. Then cut 2mm off the width and length of both door panels. Cover the smaller interior panel with the interior fabric and the exterior panel with the exterior polycotton.

2. Place the blackwork embroidery on to the exterior door panel so that the top and bottom are evenly spaced. The side the lock casing is to be joined to must have a slightly bigger gap so that the edges of the lock casing line up with the edge of the board and a vertical line of the embroidery (a small amount of embroidery will be hidden under the lock casing). Pin into place, starting with both long sides, then the straight bottom edge, and lastly the angled side so that the grain of the linen follows all of the straight edges of the board.

3. Lace the embroidery to the back of the door following the instructions in Chapter 2. Because the gap at the bottom is only a couple of millimetres there is no need to mitre the bottom corners. Remove the pins and smooth the edges of the panel with a mellor to remove any pinholes.

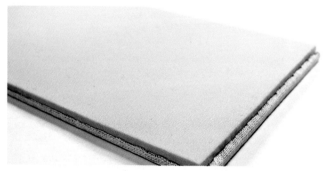

4. Place the interior door panel onto the back of the exterior door panel and, making sure that all edges except the bottom edge are flush with each other, stitch the two panels together.

5. Place the lock casing into position on the embroidered side of the door, so that it is centred between the top and bottom embroidered panels. Carefully stitch all around the casing to join it to the door, making sure that the three front sections are flush with the edge of the door.

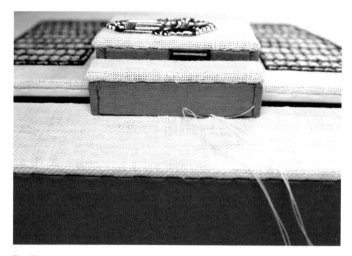

6. Place the door into the doorway, making sure that the bottom of the door is flush with the bottom edge of the box. Join the door to the box on the hinge side using buttonhole thread, making sure that the stitches go through both layers of fabric, not just the linen. There will be a slight gap to the top and side of the door to allow for ease of movement when opening and closing. By having the bottom of the door flush with the bottom of the box the door can be supported by the surface it is placed upon when opened, rather than the hinge holding the full weight of the door and lock.

7. The lock keep can then be placed into position on the exterior front strip next to the lock casing. Making sure that the deadbolt can slot into the keep, join all edges to the front strip making sure that the three front panels on the keep are flush with the edge of the doorway.

Close-up of the lock and keep on the door.

CHAPTER 8

EMBROIDERY PROJECTS FROM THE BOXES

This chapter will guide you through the embroidery projects that have been used on the boxes. They can all be adapted to suit the chosen colour theme of your box and personalized to your tastes (or those of the recipient if it is to be a gift). I have included a working order for each but not a step-by-step guide, unless the design is a smaller design. For written instructions and diagrams of the stitches please see the Stitch Glossary at the back of the book. You can find more information about the stitches and techniques in the books listed in the Further Reading section, some of which have step-by-step instructions.

PREPARING FABRIC FOR EMBROIDERY

HOW TO SET UP A SLATE FRAME

Cut the fabric you wish to frame up several inches larger than the design to be embroidered and neaten any frayed edges. Depending on the fabric used, it is advisable to pull the warp and weft threads from the edges of the fabric until you have a continuous line from one side of the fabric to the other. Threads running in the opposite direction from the pulled thread can then be trimmed back so that the edge of the fabric follows the grain along each side. For the correct tension to be maintained across the fabric it must be mounted as straight as possible on the slate frame.

You will need

- Slate frame
- Fabric for the embroidery
- Buttonhole thread
- Webbing
- Pencil
- Glass-headed and dressmaking pins
- Size 9 sharps needle
- Bracing needle
- String
- Acid-free tissue paper
- Mellor

Hints and tips

Long and short stitches are needed to secure the fabric, especially on linen, to prevent holes or too much pressure forming on one of the weft threads when the fabric is pulled tight. The stitches do not need to be particularly neat, as they are only used to secure the fabric to the frame, and a knot can be left on the top at the start since it will be removed when dismantling the frame.

The fabric can be rolled around one or both of the top and bottom frame arms to shorten the design area. This is necessary if you are going to be stitching more than one design on the same piece of fabric, to avoid having to frame up more than once.

Close-up of goldwork letter 'E' from the pentagon memory box.

1. Once the cut edges are straight, fold under the top and bottom edges by 1cm following the grain. If not already marked, using a tape measure mark the centre point on the top and bottom webbed frame arms; these are known as roller arms. Fold the fabric in half to make a small crease to mark the centre of the fabric on one of the edges. Pin from the centre out onto the underside of the webbing, on each of the roller arms, so that the raw edges (at the top and bottom) are sandwiched between the webbing and the right side of the fabric.

2. Working from the centre of the fabric out to each edge (to stop wrinkles forming), using buttonhole thread and a size 9 sharps needle, sew over the folded edge of the fabric and webbing using randomly sized long and short stitches spaced 1–2mm apart.

3. Steps 1 and 2 can then be repeated for the other end of the fabric and the remaining frame arm. As slate frames are only usually used if the design is large or will take a while to stitch, it is good practice at this point to pin two pieces of acid-free tissue paper to the reverse of the webbing with dressmaking pins so that the edge of the tissue is against the wood of the frame arm.

Hints and tips

To tighten the fabric on the frame using split pins, place the frame on the floor and using your foot put enough pressure on the end of the roller arm so that the split pin can be moved along the stretcher arm to a hole closer to the roller arm. Do the same with the opposite side so that the fabric is pulled tight and an even tension is applied on both sides. To tighten the fabric on the other type of frame, make sure that one roller arm has the wing nuts tightened fully on both sides and the opposite end has them loosened. Twist the roller arm opposite until the fabric is as tight as it can go and secure in place by tightening the wing nuts.

4. The frame arms are then attached to the stretcher arms; these will either have small holes all the way along them or just one set of holes at each end, depending on the style of frame. With the stretcher arms that have multiple holes, thread the sides through holes in the top and bottom and secure, loosely at first, with metal split pins in the small holes. The stretcher arms should be placed in mirror image to ensure an even tension when the fabric is tightened. If using the type with only one hole at each end, place the bolt at each end of the roller arms through the holes in the stretcher arms and secure in place using the wing nuts, with the fabric kept loose at this stage.

5. Place the design within the design area to make sure that there is enough of an allowance left as it is difficult to stitch if the design is too close to the arms. Make any necessary adjustments by unwinding or winding the fabric around the roller arms.

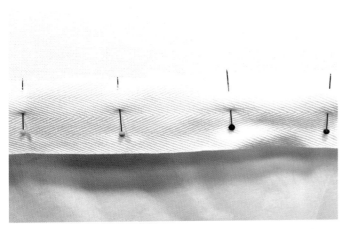

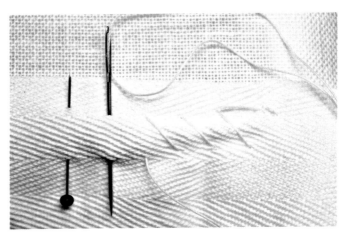

6. Once the fabric is at an even tension, the webbing needs to be cut to the length of the remaining raw sides of the fabric. The webbing is then pinned to the edge of the fabric so that three quarters of the webbing is on top of the fabric and the other quarter overhanging the edge of the fabric. The pins can be placed about an inch or so apart.

7. The webbing is then stitched to the fabric using a basting stitch with buttonhole thread and a number 5 needle; a knot can be left on the top at the start as it will be removed when dismantling the frame. The webbing will have four sections created by the weave; three of these will be over the fabric so it is best to stitch along the middle section to ensure that the fabric is caught and not so close to the edge that it might rip when tightened. The stitches should be spaced about 1cm apart and can be worked with a diagonal length either on the top or the bottom depending on which way you find more comfortable. Use a mellor to pull the stitches tight before securing the thread. Repeat this step on the opposite raw edge.

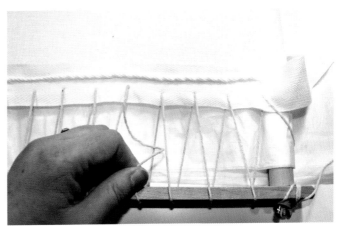

8. Thread a 5-inch bracing needle with a ball of string, which can be placed in a deep bowl or on the floor. Sew over the stretcher arms of the frame and down into the overhanging quarter of the webbing. The stitches should be placed about 1 inch apart, and the line between two woven sections on the webbing can be used as a guide. Pull through plenty of string with each stitch; more may need to be pulled through as you work the stitches along the webbing on both sides.

9. Cut the string leaving a good length at each end. Wrap one end of string around the joined ends of the arms and secure it in place with a slip knot. (A slip knot is made by loosening one of the loops of string over the join and passing the looped end of the string beneath it and pulling tight.) Then pull the loops of string along each of the stretcher arms to tighten one at a time, so that the edge of the fabric runs parallel to it.

Hints and tips

It is recommended to bind all ring frames with bias binding or strips of calico before using so that the fabric is protected from any splinters or oils in the wood. Wind the strips around each part of the hoop, securing each end of the strip with small stitches to a previous wrap of the strip. It is best to try and secure the ends on the outer edges of the two hoops, so that they will not be sandwiched between the two hoops when fitted together.

1. Bind the ring frame with strips of calico or bias binding.

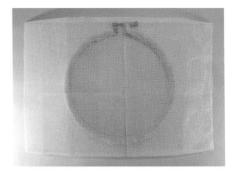

2. Cut a piece of fabric 5–10cm larger than the ring frame; place the top of the frame on the table and then place the right side of the fabric downwards on top of the ring.

3. Test the tightness of the outer ring by pressing the inner ring down on top of the fabric, if it fits inside the outer ring too easily, remove the inner ring and tighten the screw on the outer ring.

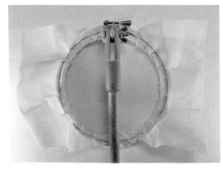

4. The outer ring is at the correct tension when some resistance is created when the inner ring is pushed inside it. The fabric should be stretched drum-tight between the two rings. The edges of the fabric can be pulled slightly in order to straighten the grain of the fabric.

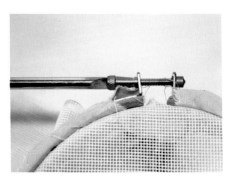

5. Using a screwdriver, tighten the screw on the outer ring once more so that the fabric is kept at the correct tension thoughout.

Design transfer

There are several methods of transferring a design onto fabric: the traditional 'prick and pounce' method; using a lightbox with pencil/pen; and also tissue paper and tacking. The traditional method of prick and pounce is a very accurate way to transfer large designs onto fabric, using a needle to prick holes along the lines of your design drawn onto tracing paper. Depending on the colour of the fabric you are using, either finely ground charcoal (for light fabrics) or finely ground dried cuttlefish (for dark fabrics) is pounced (not brushed) with a baby brush so that it falls through the pricked holes to transfer the design onto the fabric. Using a very fine paintbrush and undiluted gouache, paint over the dotted lines to mark the design permanently to the fabric. It is important not to dilute the gouache with any water so that should you need to adapt the design slightly, the paint can be carefully picked off with the end of a needle. While this is a time-consuming method for larger designs it is the best method to use because it will not fade and need to be redrawn, as a pen or pencil design might; this will save you time in the long run. When pouncing designs onto leather it is best to pounce the design onto the back rather than the front, so you will need to flip the design over and prick the back so that once the leather is cut out the design will be the correct way round.

Using a lightbox with permanent pencils, fabric pencil propelling markers or fabric-safe pens is the quickest method to transfer small designs. The lines of the design need to be dark enough to show through the fabric with the lightbox on.

1. Draw the design onto tracing paper and place on top of a scrap piece of card. Using a pricker, with size 10 needle, prick small holes along the lines of the design approximately 2–3mm apart.

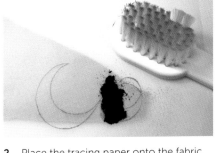

2. Place the tracing paper onto the fabric and centre the design up with the grain of the fabric (or on leather, position the design to be as economical as possible). Pounce the ground charcoal through the pricked holes using a baby brush.

Making sure that you have crossed lines in the centre of the design, line up the grain of the fabric to ensure that the design is straight on the fabric and then trace over the design using the appropriate pen or pencil. This method works best on light and thinner fabrics; you are unlikely to be able to use this for dark/black fabrics, as the design will not show through.

Tissue paper and tacking is the final method for design transfer. This is usually used for openwork designs such as blackwork or whitework, when you do not want a lined edge on the design. The design is carefully drawn onto tissue paper – a slightly blunt normal pencil is best for this, so that it does not damage the tissue. The tissue is then pinned onto the fabric and then using single lengths of sewing thread, leaving the knots on top, tack along the design using varying stitch length in order to mark the lines of the design as accurately as possible. Once the whole design has been tacked into place the tissue paper can be removed, taking care not to disturb the stitches. You may need tweezers to help remove small pieces, depending on the level of detail in your design.

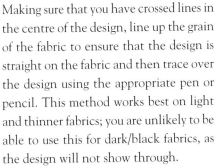

A lightbox being used to transfer a design onto canvas.

The method used to work the smocking in Chapter 5 is the same method that is used for transferring a design onto fabric with tissue paper; when transferring a design the paper is removed after the tacking stitches are completed.

HEART-SHAPED EMBROIDERY FROM CHAPTER 2

This heart has been designed using stitches to match the pattern on the fabric but can be worked in any shape. It is worked using closed loop pendant couching, whipped backstitch and beads. Closed loop pendant couching is worked in a similar way to couching but the thread is twisted to create a loop before the couching stitch, in a different colour of thread, holds it securely to the fabric. Whipped backstitch is worked as a normal backstitch, then a contrasting coloured thread is passed through each stitch using a tapestry needle. Alternative stitches can be used if you are designing a piece to match the pattern on your chosen fabric. For further information on these and other stitch techniques please refer to the Glossary and the Further Reading section.

You will need

- Exterior fabric from the box
- Lightweight calico backing
- Stranded cotton in two shades of the same colour
- Two colours of beads to match the colour of the cotton threads
- Embroidery needle
- Tapestry needle
- Beading thread
- Fabric pencil
- Fabric and embroidery scissors
- Ring frame
- Dressmaking pins

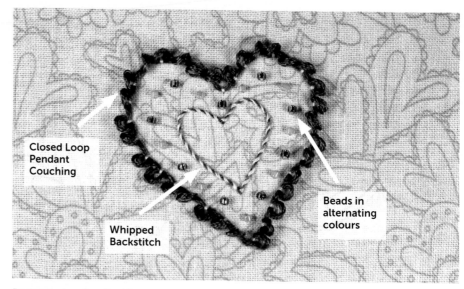

Closed Loop Pendant Couching

Whipped Backstitch

Beads in alternating colours

Design for heart embroidery.

Hints and tips

The threads can be different shades of the same colour to match the colour of the fabric or you can make them contrasting colours with matching beads. The choice of colour is entirely up to you.

WORKING ORDER

1. Place the fabric with calico backing in a ring frame and tighten to the correct tension. Transfer the design onto the fabric using a lightbox.

2. Using two colours of stranded cotton work closed loop pendant couching around the larger heart, starting at the point and working along the line of the heart.

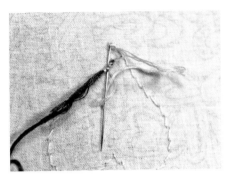

3. The ends of the couched thread need to be plunged using a lasso in a large needle and secured to the back of the fabric.

4. On the smaller heart shape, work a backstitch all the way around the design keeping the stitches as even as possible, 3–4mm long.

5. The backstitch is then whipped using two strands of different coloured thread creating a twisted cord-like effect. The thread is started and finished on the back of the fabric.

6. Place pins at even intervals in the area between the two heart shapes to work out the spacing for the beads. Count the pins to ensure that the colour of the beads can be alternated without duplicating the colour where they meet up.

7. Alternating the colour of the beads, use beading thread to stitch twice through the beads to secure them into position; remove each pin as you work around the design.

Close-up of monogrammed initials.

···⁘[PROJECT]⁘···

MONOGRAM FROM CHAPTER 4

Monograms are worked in trailing, which is similar to couching but the laid threads underneath act like padding and are completely hidden by the holding stitches worked tightly together over the top to secure the strands beneath. Traditionally, trailing is used in whitework, either as one of a number of techniques or on its own; for further information about whitework techniques please refer to the Glossary and the Further Reading section.

You will need

- Exterior fabric from the box
- Lightweight calico backing
- Stranded cotton in three very different shades of the same colour
- Fabric pencil
- Fabric and embroidery scissors
- Ring frame

Hints and tips

Try to use a font that is simple to work but also connects nicely to join up the letters in the initial you are working. This can either be done by hand, using tracing paper to overlap the letters on a lightbox, or using a computer programme that employs layers to see how they overlap to fit together. Using three very different shades of the same coloured thread is an effective way of ensuring the letters stand out but are still connected. This could also be worked in different colours to match the fabrics you have chosen to use on the box.

The thickness of the trailing line can be tailed off at the ends by cutting some of the strands beneath away before continuing along the line until all threads have been gradually cut back and the final holding stitches cover the ends; or they can be worked in the same thickness throughout and the group of laid threads all cut together at the end of the line.

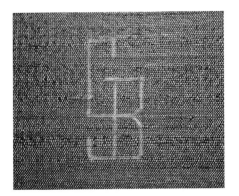

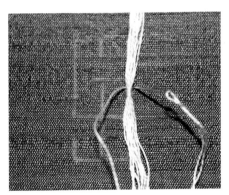

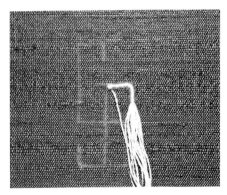

1. Place the fabric with calico backing in a ring frame and tighten to the correct tension. Transfer the design onto the fabric using a lightbox, using a thin line rather than the thickness of the finished letters so that the lines will be covered.

2. Starting in the middle of the letter that will be at the back, use stranded cotton to work trailing lines to create the parts of the letter in the first colour of thread. Depending on the letter being worked it could be created by more than one line of trailing. The number of strands used is entirely up to you depending on the thickness of line you wish to achieve; I have used twelve laid strands for this design.

3. Trailing is worked from the centre out to the end of each line for the letter being worked; it is important to angle the needle as you stitch to help create a nice curve over the laid threads.

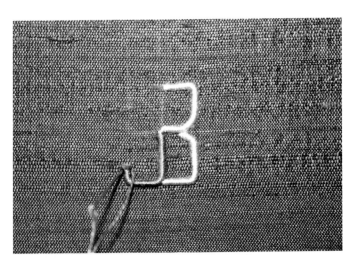

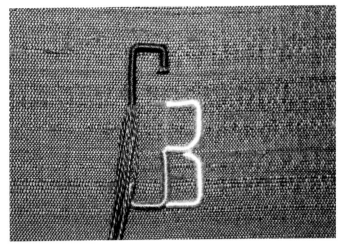

4. Once the first letter has been completed the next letter can be worked in a different shade of the thread colour. It is important that where this letter joins onto the first letter it slightly overlaps the stitching from the first letter to create a neat join.

5. The final letter is then worked in another shade of the colour; depending on the letter this can be done in one continuous length worked from the centre out. Again it is important that where this letter connects to the previous stitching there is a slight overlap to make sure that the join is neat and that the top letter sits above the others.

Design for the silk shaded crocus.

·❈[PROJECT]❈·

SILK SHADED CROCUS FROM CHAPTER 4

Silk shading or thread painting is worked in long and short stitch; however, as the name suggests, it is not necessarily worked as alternating long and short stitches with the same length. The stitches need to vary in length to help them blend in, so that although there are alternating long and short stitches they vary in length. Each section to be worked has a line of split stitches worked along the edges of the design. Where another section crosses over or joins the first section, the split stitch for the next section is worked after the long and short stitches so the split stitches will sit over the top of the long and short stitches. This makes a clear line, which helps to create a depth of field.

Silk shading is worked based on depth perception, so areas that will be further away are worked first and then the design is continued in order until the areas at the front are completed. This is sometimes not straightforward: you may find that you need to pause during the stitching of one area to start another in order to work the design in the correct order to maintain the perspective, particularly where two areas merge. If you are new to silk shading you can adapt this design so the colours are simpler, with only three or four colours

of purple, but it is important to mix the colours rather than working in rows of the same colour to avoid creating clear bands of colour. Silk shading is always worked using just one strand of each colour in a needle; you will therefore need more than one needle as the threads are often worked simultaneously picking up the colour that's needed for a few stitches and then changing to another. It is important to keep the thread length short and to replace the thread as soon as it starts looking worn; it is easier to replace a worn thread than a snapped one and your embroidery will have a finer finish. For more information on silk shading please refer to the Glossary and the Further Reading section.

You will need

- Exterior fabric from the box
- Lightweight calico backing
- Four shades of purple stranded cotton ranging from dark to light
- Purple/blue stranded cotton
- Two shades of pink stranded cotton
- Four shades of green stranded cotton
- White stranded cotton
- Three shades of yellow to orange stranded cotton
- Fabric pencil
- Fabric and embroidery scissors
- Ring frame
- Size 12 needles (or 10 if 12s are unavailable); ideally you will need one needle per colour.

Hints and tips

It is always a good idea to have a go at creating your own colour plan by blending coloured pencils so that you can gain a better understanding of which threads you may need in each section before you work the embroidery.

I find it useful to thread up needles with all of the colours I will need for each section before I start stitching because it's easier to achieve the correct mix if you have needles ready to go, just like mixing paints before you start painting. That way you won't forget to include colours that could help add depth to the embroidery.

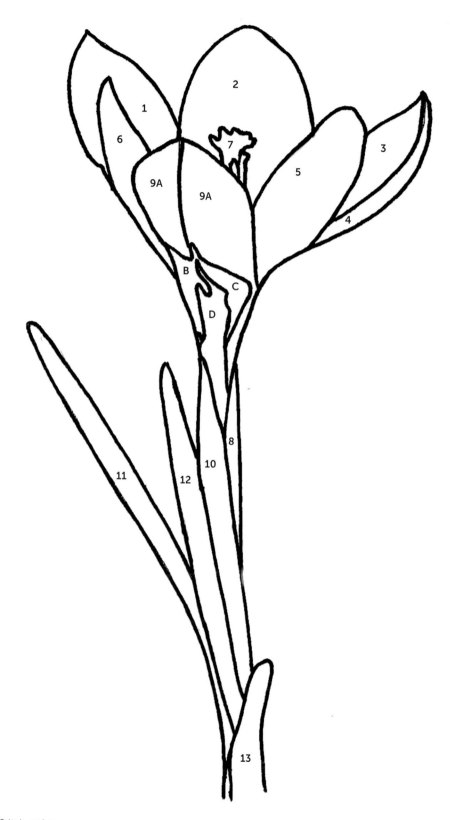

Stitch order.

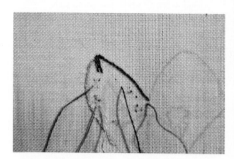

1. Place the fabric into a ring frame, tighten to the correct tension and then transfer the design onto the fabric using a light-box. Starting with petal 1, work the petals of the flower in the order marked on the stitch plan, always starting by working a split stitch along the design lines.

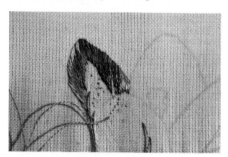

2. Blend in the colours as if you were painting to create realistic-looking shading using the colours from the photo as a guide. The four purples, two pinks, purple/blue and white stranded cottons are all used to create the shading on the petals.

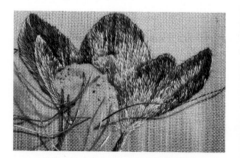

3. Continue working the petals until you complete section 6. Section 7 is the stamen at the centre of the flower, which is worked in the three threads that vary from yellow to orange. This section is very small so will need smaller stitches than those used on the petals.

4. Section 8 is part of a leaf and is worked next in two of the green threads.

5. The final petal, section 9, is worked in four parts, labelled 9A, B, C, D. 9A is started first but not completed until after B, C, D have been worked; it is a bit of a stop/start process but it's important to do it this way so that A appears to be over the top of the lower sections, which merge into the stem.

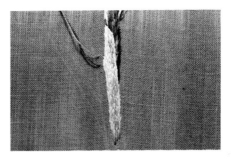

6. The stem, section 10, is worked next, blending the two pale purple threads and a white thread.

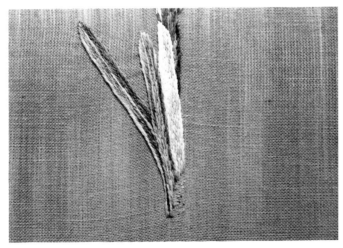

7. The two full leaves, sections 11 and 12, are worked next using all four shades of green thread.

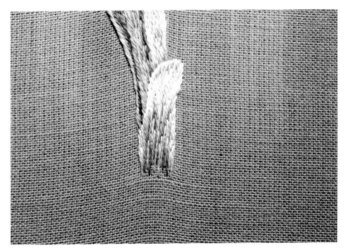

8. The final stage is to work the spathe (this protects the petals while they are growing) at the bottom of the stem. This is mainly worked in white with a few stitches in green to add extra depth.

···⋄[PROJECT]⋄···

CREWELWORK LEAF FROM CHAPTER 4

Crewelwork is traditionally wool threads worked on a linen twill fabric, but this is a very expensive fabric stocked by only a few suppliers. It is becoming more popular to use other alternatives such as plain linen or linen-effect fabrics with patterns. For this project I decided to use a patterned linen-effect fabric because I wanted to use the same fabric on all of the exterior panels and not just the lid. I thought it would look a bit plain with an unpatterned fabric so my choice is, I think, a compromise between traditional and modern fabrics. I have used trellis, slanted satin, heavy chain, French knots and couching in this design. For more information on these stitches and others used in crewelwork please see the Glossary and the Further Reading section.

You will need

- Exterior fabric from the box
- Green crewel wool: light and dark
- Pink crewel wool
- Fabric pencil
- Fabric and embroidery scissors
- Ring frame
- Chenille needle

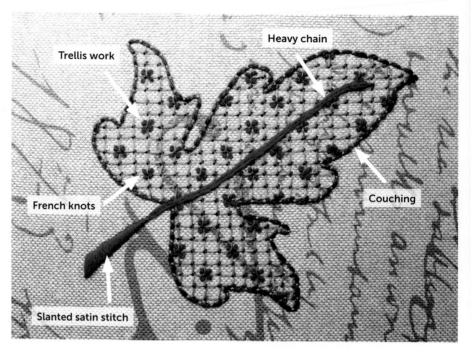

Crewelwork leaf.

WORKING ORDER

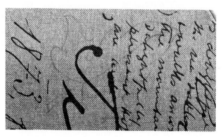

1. Place the fabric in a ring frame and tighten to the correct tension. Transfer the design onto the fabric using a lightbox.

3. Then work the vertical bars, again working from the centre out, keeping the bar spacing the same as the horizontal bars.

2. Start by working the horizontal bars for the trellis, following the grain of the fabric; the bars are worked back and forth from the centre out with the spacing kept as even as possible. After the first bar has been made the stitch is carried under the fabric and the needle brought to the top on the same side of the design. This is so that there are small thread trails at the back, rather than long lengths carried across the back to the other side of the design; this saves wasting thread where it won't be seen.

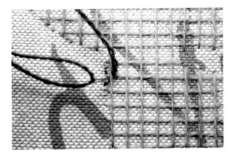

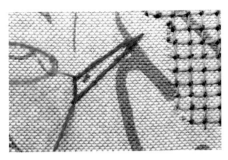

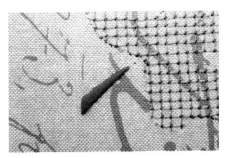

4. Small diagonal (bottom left to top right) stitches are placed over the bars where the two sets of bars cross over to hold the bars in the correct position.

5. Split stitch is then worked around the end section of the leaf stem.

6. Slanted satin is worked along the end of the stem using the split stitch as a guide to achieve an evenly stitched edge.

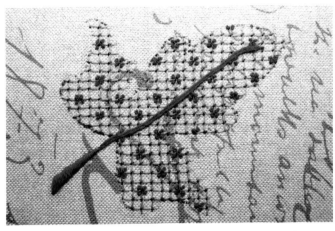

7. Starting at the other end of the stem, work a heavy chain stitch along the line of the stem, ending where it joins the slanted satin stitch.

8. French knots are then worked in a pattern grouping together at the cross-over section in four squares followed by a gap of four empty squares. This pattern can be started at any point but needs to be continued throughout the leaf shape.

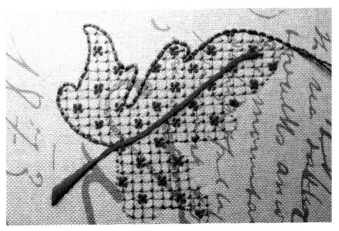

9. Two couched lines are then worked around the edges of the leaf, starting at the bottom of each side and working around to the tip. The couched threads can be started individually with a holding stitch and joined together in the same hole at the start of the couched line.

10. The two ends of the couched lines at the tip are then plunged to give a neat point to the leaf and secured on the back of the fabric.

CANVAS EMBROIDERY FROM CHAPTER 5

Canvas embroidery is traditionally wool threads worked on either a single or double canvas with stitches in a set pattern or mixed together to create the design. Canvas is strong and has evenly spaced, open holes that are clearly visible so it is easy to count the threads for the stitch being worked. Canvas can be embroidered using other threads but the number of strands of each thread needed will depend on the size of the canvas; the threads need to cover the threads of the canvas without distorting their spacing.

For this design I have used Florentine stitch to create a pattern that is similar to that of the fabric used on the rest of the box and I have selected complementary colours. This pattern can be adapted depending on the thread count of your canvas and the style of the fabric you are using for the rest of the box. Florentine stitch is worked in straight stitches over four threads of the canvas. The order that they are stitched depends on the shape of the pattern than you are working: they can be side by side or drop down by 1–4 threads.

Canvas embroidery.

WORKING ORDER

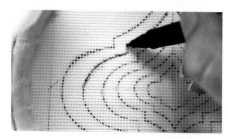

1. Using a lightbox and a permanent marker pen, draw the line guide onto the canvas. Place the canvas in a ring frame and tighten to the correct tension.

2. Working from the centre of the design, work Florentine stitch from the pen line and count up four threads. Start with a knot on top and the first stitch started at least an inch away so that the thread is caught by the stitches that are then worked up to the knot.

You will need

• Canvas
• Various colours of perlé thread or stranded cotton
• Permanent marker
• Fabric and embroidery scissors
• Ring frame
• Tapestry needle

3. Continue along the pen line so that the bottoms of the stitches follow the pen line until you reach each edge of the design area. When you have finished with a thread it is brought up at least an inch away from the final stitch and the end left on top until it has been worked up to and is secure.

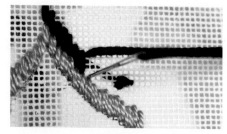

4. Once the first line is complete, continue working Florentine stitch matching the pattern from the first line and alternating the colours so that they are in the same sequence throughout.

PROJECT

GOLDWORK LETTER 'E' FROM CHAPTER 6

Goldwork is a lovely technique to work because it not only looks impressive but it also adds a bit of glamour to your work. It can be worked on almost any fabric with a calico backing to add support and leather can be used to fill in larger areas quickly. This design uses leather appliqué, cutwork and pearl purl and can be adapted for use with any letter or font style. Leather appliqué involves cut pieces of leather (either metallic or coloured) applied to the fabric with small stitches to keep it secured while other techniques are worked. Cutwork uses string padding with rough or bright check worked over the top at a 45° angle to create an 'S'

shape which sits neatly against the padding and does not create a loop above it. Pearl purl is used to edge the leather to cover the small stitches and create a neat edge, which can also be continued to add little teardrop-shaped details at the end of the letters.

You will need

- Fabric from the exterior of the box
- Lightweight calico
- Metallic leather for goldwork
- Goldwork cotton string
- Rough and bright check purl
- Pearl purl
- Beeswax
- Machine sewing thread
- Fabric, embroidery and goldwork scissors
- Mellor
- Ring frame
- Size 10 or 12 needle
- Charcoal pounce

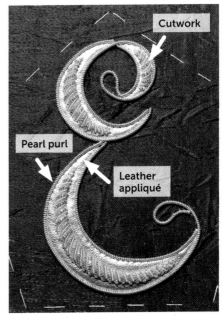

Goldwork letter E with leather appliqué, pearl purl and cutwork.

WORKING ORDER

1. Place the exterior fabric with the calico backing in a ring frame. Taking the cut-out panel of card for the lid, use a pencil to trace around it on the calico at the back of the ring frame.

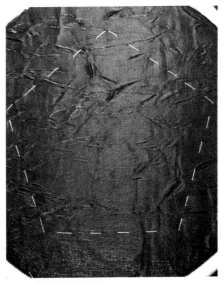

2. Using a contrasting colour of machine sewing thread, tack along the pencil line using large stitches to create an outline of the lid on the exterior fabric.

3. Pricking the wrong side of the design, pounce the design onto the back of the leather so that the letter will be the correct way round once cut from the leather. The parts of the letter are to be attached separately so they can be pounced individually to be economical with the leather. Then draw around the shapes with pencil.

4. Cut the leather shapes out with curved embroidery scissors and then position on the fabric using the original design as a guide. Unless your font is more complex it's not necessary to draw the design onto the fabric; this helps to avoid unwanted design lines that can't be covered later.

5. Start working around each shape with small stab stitches: bring the needle up next to the leather shape and stitch down into it about 1–2mm from the edge. Place the stitches about 1cm apart to hold the leather in place while you work on the other shapes.

6. Once you are happy with the position of all the shapes you can work around them again with more stab stitches, this time about 2–3mm apart.

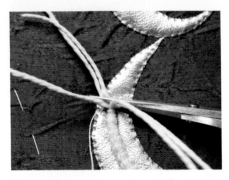

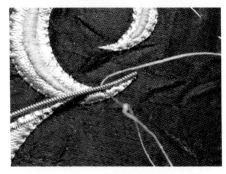

7. The waxed string padding is now applied to the centre of each of the leather shapes, working from the centre of each shape and using 12 lengths for the large bottom section, 8 for the middle, and 3 for the small top section. The string padding is gradually cut down to taper each end to a narrow point. Oversew with waxed sewing thread to hold in place.

8. The pearl purl edge is worked next, making sure that it has been stretched slightly and a whole twist is visible at the start. The end is secured with two stitches of waxed thread. Continue working along the pearl purl, stitching down every 3–4 twists with a slight back stitch and angling the needle to make sure the stitch is hidden. The end is cut between the twists so that a whole twist is visible and then secured with two stitches before the final twist.

9. Gentle curves can be worked freehand; tighter twists and teardrop shapes will need to be guided into place using a mellor before being secured with stitches. The end is cut before the final securing stitches with the scissors following the direction of the twist to leave a whole twist once cut, then the end is secured with two stitches, as at the beginning.

10. Cutwork is then worked over the top of the string padding, working from the centre out to each end, using a mellor to guide the cut rough and bright check lengths into place, alternating along the design. The cut pieces should form an 'S' shape across the padding. Working up towards the top, the stitches are worked top to bottom, angling the needle to place the end of the length being secured as close to the previous piece as possible without damaging it. Working down to the end of the line, the cut pieces are stitched from bottom to top, again angling the needle to tuck the end in close to the previous piece.

··❧[PROJECT]❧··

STUMPWORK FLOWER PETALS FROM CHAPTER 6

Stumpwork, like goldwork, is equally impressive, particularly when used to create separate 3D elements that are later added to the fabric. Stumpwork can be used to add height to your box, which is particularly useful for small boxes. There are various ways to incorporate stumpwork into your designs but for this project I decided that individual wired fabric slip flower petals would work best with the size of the box. They can be time-consuming to make but because they can be worked in a small ring frame they are easy to pick up and transportable.

Design plan for stumpwork flower petals.

Hints and tips

The petals can be worked using more than one colour of thread but I suggest that you work out a pattern for the colours prior to stitching the petals. As long as there isn't a pattern on the fabric and the petals follow the grain they can be positioned on the fabric to be as economical as possible but remember to allow enough space between, so that you don't risk cutting the stitches when cutting them out from the fabric.

You will need

- Fabric for the petals
- Fine white cake wire
- Darker colour of stranded cotton to match the colour of the petal fabric
- Fabric, embroidery and goldwork scissors
- Mellor
- Ring frame
- Size 10 or 12 needle
- Paper template for the petal shape
- Fabric pencil

WORKING ORDER

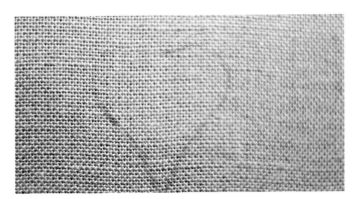

1. Place the petal fabric in a small ring frame and using a fabric pencil trace around the template.

2. Cut a length of the cake wire in half (using your goldwork scissors). Lay the wire along the pencil line, leaving at least an inch or more of the wire as a tail. Then, using a single strand of thread, work a holding stitch at the start and secure with a second stitch on top of the first.

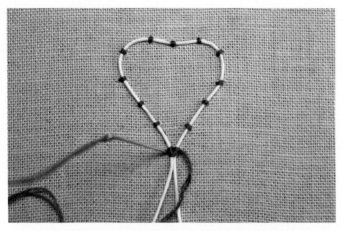

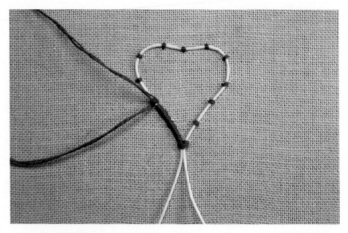

3. Continue with small stitches spaced about 3–4mm apart securing the wire, bending it around to follow the curve (a mellor can help with this). Where the wires meet, place a couple of small stitches over them to hold them together so they are positioned side by side.

4. Now that the wire is secured in place it needs to be covered by trailing with two strands over the wire, filling in the gaps between the securing stitches and ensuring that the white of the wire is not visible.

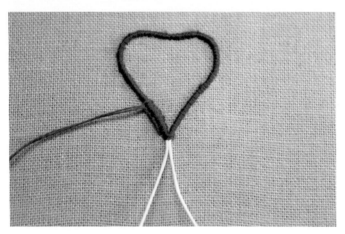

5. Using two strands of the thread in the needle, work buttonhole stitch tightly over the wire with the loop on the outside edge of the petal.

6. Repeat steps 1–5 until you have the desired number of petals – fifteen in this case, so there are five for each flower. When you have enough petals the fabric can be removed from the frame and the petals carefully cut from the fabric using a fine pair of scissors, curved if possible to help avoid cutting any stitches by accident. The instructions for grouping the petals together on the fabric for the lid are in Chapter 6.

PROJECT
SMOCKING
FROM CHAPTER 7

Smocking is worked using various methods: either by working stitches on pre-pleated fabric to create a pattern holding the pleats in place, or by stitching the fabric in a set order to create pleats in the fabric. For this particular project I have used a form of Canadian smocking with beads; this means that you do not need to have a special pleating machine to work it. I used squared paper to create a bricked pattern which was then stitched in rows, threading beads on the stitches on the right side of the fabric which when pulled tight would form a honeycomb pattern. Using large beads and stitches meant that the pleats created were larger, which made mounting easier – forming the folds into neat pleats on the top and bottom of the fabric. The order of the bead colours is entirely up to you: the pattern can be as simple or complicated as you wish.

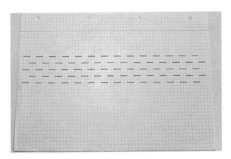

Design plan for smocking using squared paper.

Hints and tips

Before you start on the main fabric you may want to do a test on calico: stitch a couple of rows 10cm or so long to see how much the fabric reduces by to work out how long each row needs to be to fit your box. You can use squared paper to create your own template to fit the size of beads or pearls you are using and the size of your box.

You will need

- Exterior fabric
- Sewing thread
- Large beads or faux pearls in two colours
- Fabric and embroidery scissors
- Mellor
- Tweezers
- Size 10 or 12 needle
- Tissue paper
- Fabric pencil

WORKING ORDER

1. Trace the design onto tissue paper using a ruler and a soft fabric pencil so as not to tear the paper.

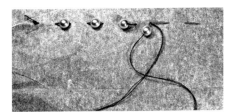

3. Starting with a secure knot, work a running stitch with a long double length of sewing thread. Thread a bead onto the needle before every stitch is worked on the right side of the fabric so that the bead sits between each pencil line marked onto the tissue paper. Leave the thread at the end of each row.

2. Pin the tissue paper onto the exterior fabric so that the stitch lines follow the grain of the fabric.

4. Once all of the rows have been stitched the tissue can be removed from the fabric by carefully tearing it to release it from the stitches.

5. Pull the thread on each of the rows to gather up the fabric and beads, making sure that the thread is on the back of the fabric so that the ends can be tied together and then secured with a holding stitch behind a bead.

BLACKWORK FROM CHAPTER 7

Blackwork is traditionally worked on even-weave linen and is worked in a wide variety of counted stitch patterns. These originally would have been worked using the same thickness of thread throughout but over the years have been developed in order to create shading. The thickness or number of threads used can be changed in order to create a depth to your work. The stitch used will also increase or decrease the amount of light or dark in the design: smaller patterns will look darker and open patterns will make the area lighter. The patterns can be broken up to create even more light or worked in a variety of thread thicknesses in the same area of the design to add even more detail. This project uses two strands of cotton, one strand of cotton, and machine sewing thread to create the texture for the wooden planks on the door. This is the advantage of blackwork over other techniques: the counted patterns can be adapted to fit in with the pattern or texture of the design you are trying to create and detail can be added with shading.

Before working your design you would usually work a detailed shading plan but for this piece I decided to shade randomly to create the texture of wood and have chosen to use interlocking 'Y's, which look a bit like the knots in wood. You would also usually keep continuity of the pattern across the whole area to be worked in the same stitch but I have deliberately decided to restart the pattern on each plank to make sure that they are clearly separate from each other. Outlines would also usually be left until last but in this case

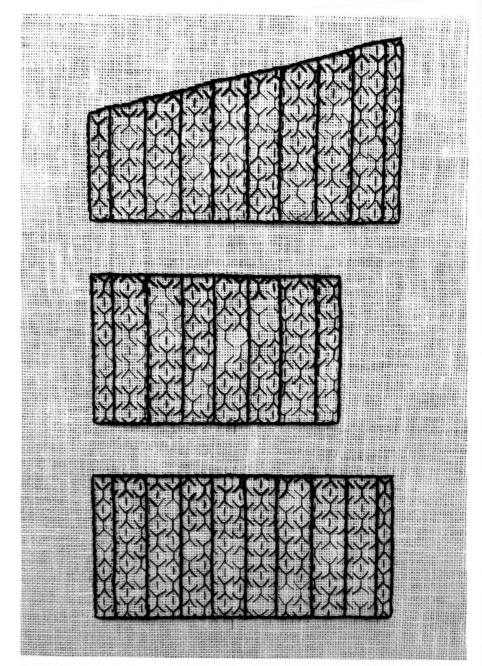

The blackwork door from the wedding card box.

it helps to create a defined line between each plank section making sure that the pattern stays within each plank. The pattern is worked over three threads of the linen; because the shading is worked in different threads there is no set way to stitch this pattern other than keeping to the number of threads it is worked across, which is why I haven't included a stitch diagram. The photographs in the step-by-step should be enough of a guide. It is best with this design to use a slate frame because of its size and the time that it will take to embroider.

You will need

- White even-weave linen fabric (32 TPI)
- Black and pale blue sewing thread
- Black stranded cotton
- Fabric and embroidery
- Mellor
- Tweezers
- Fine tapestry needle
- Fabric pencil
- Tissue paper
- Slate frame

1. Frame the fabric in a slate frame following the instructions at the beginning of this chapter and work a tacking line in a pale blue sewing thread. Using a lightbox, mark on the three areas of the door to be stitched using the design as a guide. Be sure to follow a thread up so that the areas are perfectly straight to the grain; I would only mark on the corners and top or bottom of the vertical lines as the threads will act as enough of a guide.

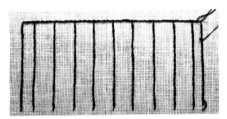

3. The top horizontal line is then worked, cutting off any ends of threads as you reach them, as long as they are secure. The other end is left open for the threads from the pattern; they can be removed at the end once fully secure.

2. Starting with the bottom set of planks, work the stem stitch vertical lines using two strands of cotton; leave a knot about an inch away on top and stitch up to it before cutting the knot off.

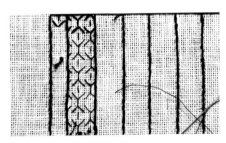

4. The interlocking 'Y's stitch can then be worked with three needles set up for one or two strands and also sewing thread. It is best to start with a full-sized plank; the stitch is worked across three threads of the linen and it is important to try and work the stitches in order to avoid trailing too much of the threads behind it.

6. The bottom horizontal line can then be worked in stem stitch so that the ends of the thread can be removed. Any that aren't fully secure should be taken to the back and worked into the stitches on the back, using a lasso of thread if it's too short to use with the needle.

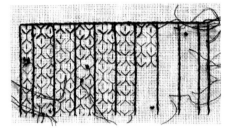

5. Continue working the plank sections, varying the shading and starting position of the stitch based on the previous planks so that the shading creates a mottled effect over the panel. Every new thread should be started with a knot away from the area to be stitched and only removed once the thread is secure; no stitches should move when pulled.

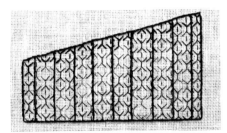

7. Repeat steps two to six on the other two panels, making sure that all edges follow the same thread line from the bottom to the top section. The top of the angled panel will be the only edge not worked following a grain line from one side to the other.

Design plan for the rabbit and roses.

WHITEWORK AND RIBBONWORK FROM CHAPTER 7

Whitework is also worked on even-weave linen using various different stitches and techniques: pulled work, drawn threads and counted stitches are some of these. It can be combined with other techniques worked in white threads, such as stump-work or ribbonwork, to give extra depth to the design. For this project design I decided to combine ribbonwork and pulled work to create the white rabbit and roses. The linen for this design was framed up in a slate frame allowing enough fabric for both this design and the blackwork door to save having to frame up twice; the blackwork was worked first. If you are

Hints and tips

With ribbonwork you can leave the knot on the back and also carry the ribbon across the back depending on the fabric and method of mounting. Because the linen is mounted on a blue fabric it is important to make sure no threads are carried across the back and all ends are secured with stitches rather than knots to stop the linen from becoming uneven when mounted.

only working this design you will need to frame up the fabric in a slate frame first following the instructions at the start of this chapter.

The roses are woven wheels worked in three sizes of ribbon with the buds in detached chain, and stems worked in stem stitch, also in ribbon. The rabbit's body is worked in a wave stitch filling and his ears

You will need

- White even-weave linen fabric (32 TPI)
- White and pale blue sewing thread
- White stranded cotton
- White coton floche
- White silk ribbon in 7mm, 4mm and 2mm
- Fabric and embroidery scissors
- Mellor
- Tweezers
- Chenille needle
- Size 10/12 embroidery needle
- Fine tapestry needle
- Pale blue fabric pencil
- Slate frame
- Tissue paper

and leg in a honeycomb darning stitch. His eye is padded satin, whiskers are long stitches and he is outlined with couching. It is best with this design to use a slate frame because of its size and the time that it will take to embroider.

WORKING ORDER

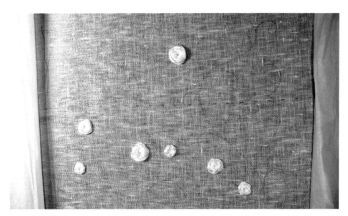

1. Use a lightbox to trace the design lines with a fabric pencil, using a metric circle guide for the three sizes of rose. Start with a woven wheel rose first. Stitch the five bars using a single thread of stranded cotton. The bars should start just beyond the pencil line and be stitched down in the centre of the circle. Continue working all the roses in three different sizes: small in the 2mm, medium in the 4mm and large in the 7mm ribbon.

2. The ends of the ribbon should be secured to the linen behind the rose, rather than leaving a knot, so that the ends are not visible once the project is mounted.

3. The buds are then worked in detached chain stitch with the 4mm ribbon followed by the vines worked in stem stitch with the 2mm ribbon; make sure the vines end on the same grain line.

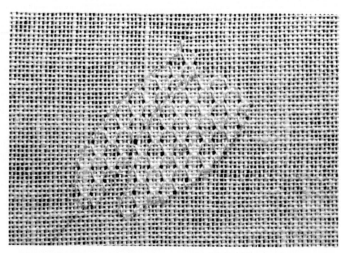

4. The rabbit's ears and leg are worked with the honeycomb darning stitch in one strand of cotton. As with the blackwork, to give a sense of depth the pattern should be started in a different place on each ear so that the pattern is not continuous from one to the other. Vary where the pattern ends where the ears meet the head so that the stitches from the rest of the body can be merged together.

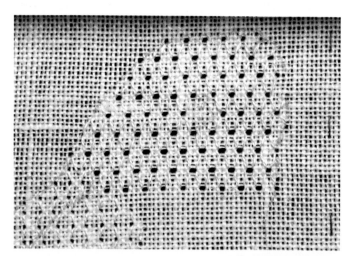

5. The main part of the body is then worked in wave stitch filling, leaving a space for the eye to be worked in padded satin stitch.

6. Once the wave stitch filling on the main part of the body is complete, a split stitch edge can be worked around the area for the eye.

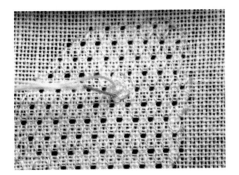

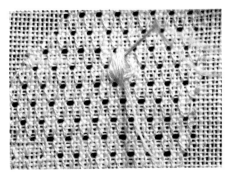

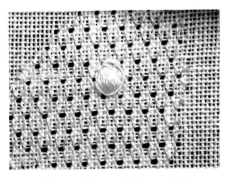

7. The padding for the eye is worked using coton floche: firstly in small stitches horizontally and then vertically over the top, alternating and increasing the stitch size and number of stitches each time until the area to be padded is filled with the stitches worked in a horizontal direction.

8. Using stranded cotton, work vertical stitches over the top of the padding from the outside of the split stitch until all of the padding and split stitch has been covered.

9. Work a small stem stitch around the eye to give it a neat outline and more detail.

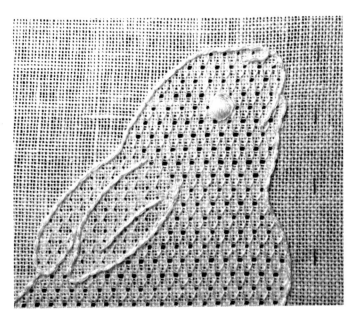

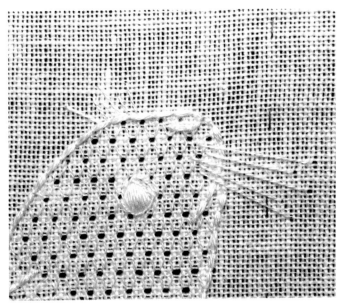

10. Outline the rabbit and the ground with couching using four strands of cotton thread. Plunge and secure by oversewing all the ends to the back of the rabbit so that they sit behind the couched lines.

11. The whiskers are straight stitches, worked freehand using a single strand of thread.

GOLDWORK AND RIBBONWORK HEXAGON FROM CHAPTER 9

Goldwork and ribbonwork make a lovely design for a box and because the ribbon can be worked over the gold thread it is possible to pack in a lot of different stitches without damaging the gold threads. The design plan for the ribbonwork flowers is a rough guide only and the number of flowers worked and their placement is entirely up to you – please adapt the plan to your tastes.

You will need

- Exterior fabric from the box
- Gilt pearl purl
- 2mm gilt spangles
- Stranded cotton to match the fabric
- Stranded cotton to match the ribbons
- Small crystal beads
- Various colours of silk ribbon in 4mm and 2mm
- Fabric and embroidery scissors
- Mellor
- Tweezers
- Chenille needle
- Size 10/12 embroidery needle
- Small metal ruler

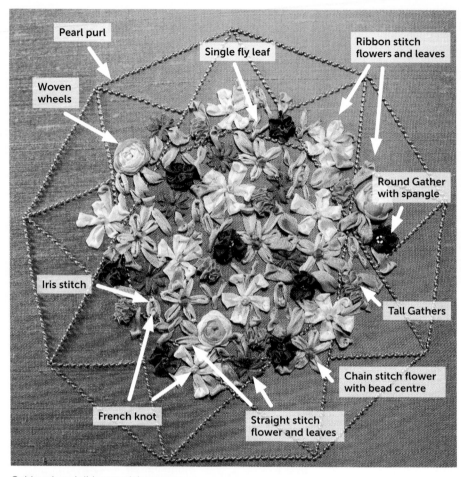

Goldwork and ribbonwork hexagon.

WORKING ORDER

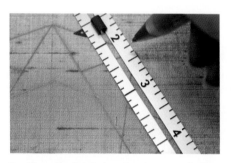

1. Place the fabric in a ring frame and using a fabric pencil and a metal ruler transfer the lines of the design onto the fabric.

2. The pearl purl is worked first around the outside edge. Over-stretch the pearl purl so that there are clear gaps between each twist for the thread to sit in. Stitches are worked in two strands of cotton matching the colour of the fabric as closely as possible. The pearl purl is stitched so the stitches are placed every two twists except at the ends, which need to be secured fully. Use a mellor to guide the pearl purl around the outside edges to get as sharp a turn as possible without distorting the gold thread.

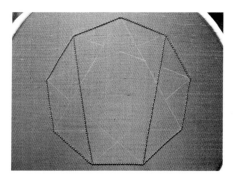

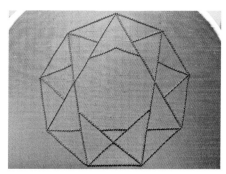

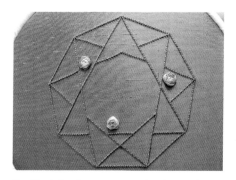

3. Once back at the start, cut the pearl purl following the twist so that once cut the end joins up with the start, and secure the end with a final stitch. Start working on the inside lines next, working the longest continuous lines first so there are as few joins as possible.

4. Continue stitching down the pearl purl lines until they have all been completed to cover the pencil lines.

5. Work the three woven wheel roses in variegated colours of 4mm ribbon. (See step 1 in the previous instructions for the whitework and ribbonwork design from Chapter 7, and the stitch glossary for this and the following ribbonwork stitches.)

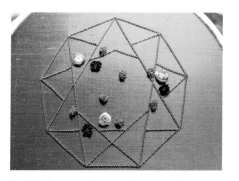

6. Work a round gather in a 4mm ribbon near each of the roses with a spangle in the centre to secure it in place. Tall gathers are worked next in a different coloured 4mm ribbon scattered around the design using the design plan as a guide.

7. Iris stitch is worked next in a 4mm ribbon with a French knot centre. Detached chain flowers are then worked in a different colour of 4mm ribbon using your stitch plan as a guide for placement.

8. Ribbon stitch flowers are then worked in a 4mm ribbon followed by straight stitch flowers with nine petals using a 2mm ribbon. Even up the design with some more iris stitch and round gather flowers.

9. Leaves are added in the spaces using straight stitches, ribbon stitch and single fly stitch. Secure small crystals in the centre of the detached chain flowers.

CHAPTER 9

ADVANCED PROJECTS
WITH MULTIPLE LEVELS AND LARGER BOXES

Once you have mastered the construction methods from the previous chapters you may wish to create a box combining several of the styles in a box with multiple levels. This will not necessarily be larger than your previous boxes but the construction will be more time-consuming and will require a bit more planning to make sure that each element is constructed in the correct order.

If you are using drawers it is important to construct these first and then their casings, even if they aren't at the bottom of the box. All other measurements will be worked out around the drawers and their casing measurements. Interior panels are constructed first; they will usually have the same width and depth measurement so it is important to keep a record of the sizes as you go. The levels can either be joined together as soon as two are completed or they can be joined once all the levels are completed but the exterior sec-

tions will not be added until the very end. If dividers or a ring holder are also to be included within the design then the order of creation will depend on where it will be placed; the dividers within a drawer will be constructed first as part of the interior drawer construction. If dividers or ring holders are to be included elsewhere then the drawer is still completed first and the dividers worked into the construction of the other levels. Deduct the thickness of the sides of the divider sections (or ring holder) from the interior measurements of the drawer casing, as it is important that the main interior panels for each level remain the same.

Cupboards can be created as part of the interior levels but the doors are best left to be completed at the end once all other elements have been constructed to ensure an accurate fit. If the top level is to be a tray or larger box section on top of

a drawer or cupboard then you will need to inset the interior panel of the tray/box above the lower drawer level. The interior panel would need to sit inside the base of the tier by the thickness of an exterior panel because the exterior panel should sit flush with the end of the interior side and top/base panels of the drawer or cupboard where the opening is.

Depending on the depth of the tray/top level of the box, it should be possible to use most lid types on a multi-level box – or none at all if you choose to have a cupboard or drawer at the top. Even if you do not have a lid, the exterior top can still be mounted with embroidery. If you are incorporating a ring holder into your design this will either need to be inset so the sides are higher than the top of the holder panels or a deeper lid used in order to leave enough space for the ring to sit above the holder.

Large jewellery box with multiple tiers including hinged two-colour lid, with ring holder tray, cupboards and drawer.

LARGE JEWELLERY BOX

It is very important to have a detailed design plan for this box because it is made up of three separate sections, which are built starting with the bottom drawer and then worked up one tier at a time to the top tray, then encased with exterior panels before the lid is constructed to fit on top. Decide on the approximate width, height and depth measurements of the overall box and divide the height into three tiers (drawer, cupboard and tray).

Large jewellery box closed with goldwork and ribbonwork embroidered lid.

You will need

- Conservation board
- Two colours of silk for the exterior/interior
- Quilting cotton for the interior
- Lightweight calico for backing the embroidery
- Cotton bump
- Sewing and buttonhole thread
- Ribbon for the lid
- Narrow double-sided tape
- Glue
- Acid-free tissue paper
- Propelling pencil
- Metal ruler
- Set square
- Stanley knife
- Cutting mat
- Embroidery and fabric scissors
- Fine curved needle
- Pins
- Small clamps
- Hand drill
- Small handles (the ones used on this box are handmade using polymer clay and small nuts and bolts)

CONSTRUCTING THE DRAWER

1. Use your design plan to work out the width, depth and height of the drawer by taking 12–13mm off the width, 6–7mm off the depth and 12–13mm off the height of the drawer tier. Cut out the interior front and back, taking a further 6mm off the length. Then cut side panels, taking 12mm off. Reduce the depth of all panels by 3mm; cover all four panels with the interior fabric.

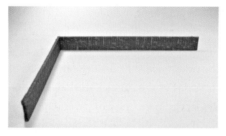

2. Join the back panel to one of the side panels so that the wrong side of the side panel sits flush with the end of the back panel.

3. The second side panel is then joined to the other end of the back panel in the same way as the first side.

4. The front panel is joined to both side panels so that the wrong side of the side panels sits flush with each end of the front panel.

5. Measure the width and depth of the interior drawer frame and cut and cover a base panel in the interior fabric. Join the base to the joined interior panels on all sides.

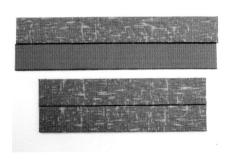

6. Using a stiletto, carefully push and twist it through the board and interior fabric to make a hole large enough for the screw from the drawer handle to fit through the centre of the drawer. The stiletto should be pushed through from both sides in order to make the hole even (rather than following the tapered shape of the stiletto).

7. Cut out four exterior panels, all 3mm deeper than the constructed interior panels, including the depth of the base panel. Start with an exterior back for the drawer 6mm larger than the interior back and cover with the interior fabric; then an exterior front which is the same size as the exterior back and cover with the exterior silk fabric. Cut two side panels the same width as the joined interior sides and cover with the interior fabric.

8. Place the exterior front underneath the interior front of the drawer so that there is a 3mm gap at each end; using the stiletto, mark the position of the hole onto the exterior front. In the same way as the interior front, push the stiletto through the board, being careful not to damage the silk, to make a hole large enough for the screw of the drawer handle.

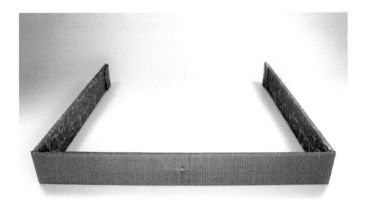

9. Join the front panel to one of the side panels so that the right side of the side panel sits flush with the end of the front panel. Join the second side panel to the other end of the front panel in the same way as the first side.

10. The back panel is joined to one of the side panels so that the right side of the side panel sits flush with each end of the front panel. Wrap the exterior sides around the constructed interior and join the last two ends together.

11. Stitch around the top edges of all interior and exterior panels to join them together so that the top edges are flush with each other.

12. Check that the measurement for the interior base, which will be placed within the interior edges of the exterior panels, is the same width and depth as the base of the interior drawer frame and cut and cover a base panel in the interior fabric. Place the base within the gap left between the exterior panels and join the base to the internal edges of the exterior panels on all sides so that the base is flush with the bottom of each panel.

13. Use the stiletto to reopen the hole if the fabric has closed up slightly while the panels were constructed.

14. Using a small screwdriver, carefully insert the screw from the interior of the drawer to the exterior in order to attach the handle.

15. Screw the handle onto the exterior side of the drawer.

1. Measure the final dimensions of the drawer, and cut out a top and base for the drawer casing, which is approximately 10mm wider and 8mm deeper than the drawer (this includes allowances for the thickness of the sides which will be joined within the area of the top and base plus 1–2mm for ease of movement). Two sides should be cut 3mm shorter than the depth of the top\base and 1–2mm higher than the external sides of the drawer. Cut a back panel the same length as the width of the top/base and the same depth as the sides; cover all panels with the interior cotton fabric.

2. Join the back panel to one of the side panels so that the end of the side panel sits the right side of the back panel.

3. The joined side and back panels are then placed on the drawer casing base so that both unjoined ends are flush with the exterior edges of the base and then stitched into place.

4. The second side is then joined onto the other end of the back panel and the base.

5. The top is placed onto the joined sides and back and joined on all three sides.

6. Check that the drawer fits easily within the casing and can be removed smoothly. Make any size adjustments now if necessary, as measurements from this tier will be repeated.

1. Cut a base and top the same size as the top and base from the drawer casing. Using the tier height measurement from the overall plan created at the start, cut two sides and two centre supports so they are the desired height of the tier minus 6mm (the thickness of the top and base) by the depth of the base minus 3mm. Cut a back panel the same height as the sides and centre supports by the width of the base/top panels. Cover all panels with the interior cotton fabric.

2. Place the two centre supports wrong sides together and ladder stitch them together around all edges.

3. Mark the centre of the base width with pins on both front and back edges. Place the centre support onto the base so that the pins sit between the two joined supports. Stitch into place around all base edges of the centre supports to join it to the base. There will be a 3mm gap on the back edge between the end of the support and the base.

4. The back is then placed onto the base so that it sits within the gap left behind the centre support. Check that the top of the support is centred with the back and pin to temporarily hold in place. Join the back to the base along the bottom edge. Double-check that the centre support hasn't shifted position while the back was joined to the base and then stitch the centre support to the back just on the top edge where they meet.

5. Join both of the sides to the back and base so that the front edge of the sides is flush with the front edge of the base panel and the other edge sits against the back panel.

6. Place the top onto the constructed parts and stitch into place on all three sides.

7. Making sure that the centre support is centred between the two sides, secure to the top along the front edge only.

8. Place the cupboard tier on top of the drawer casing and stitch together the drawer top and the cupboard base on all four edges.

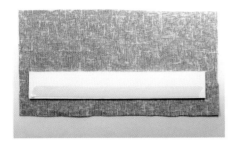

1. Using the width measurement of the cupboard top minus 6mm, cut out two panels of board for the ring holder by the desired height of the tray tier minus 3mm for the base. Cut out a piece of the interior cotton fabric with the usual allowance on three sides and an extra allowance on one long side so that the fabric can be folded over to cover the back of the board. Place tape only along the bottom edge leaving a gap of approximately 2mm between the tape and the edge of the board.

2. Stick the bottom edge of the fabric to the tape and then fold in the side edges and pin in place.

3. Fold over the larger flap so that the side edges are tucked under the fold and the side folds are flush with the side edges of the board. The raw edge of the long side is also folded back under the cover flap so that the folded edge is in line with the edge of the board. Pin the corner to hold the folded sections in place.

4. Continue to pin along the length of the panel so that the folded flap covers the wrong side of the panel and the fold follows the edge of the board.

5. Stitch the fold on all three edges to the fabric beneath; slightly larger stitches can be used because they will not be seen when joined with the other side.

6. Repeat steps 2–5 with the second ring holder panel.

7. Using the same measurements for the other top/base panels, cut out a base panel for the tray and cover with the interior cotton fabric. Mark the centre of each width side (shorter side) with a pin. Join the two ring holder panels together at one of the short ends and then place on the centre pins of the base so that the pin is in the middle of the two panels and there is a 3mm gap at each end of the panels before the edge of the base. Continue to stitch around the bottom edge of the ring holder panels to join them to the base.

8. When you reach the other end of the ring holders, stitch up and back down the other end to join the two ends together and then continue to stitch along the other bottom edge to join all bottom edges to the base.

9. Cut and cover two side panels the length of the width minus 3mm by the same depth as the ring holder panels. Place one panel in the gap left at one of the ends of the ring holder and join to the base so that there is a 3mm gap left at one end.

10. Making sure that the ring holder is centred with the side panel, join the end of the ring holder to the side panel just on the top edges, making sure that there are no holding stitches visible by securing to the wrong side of the side panel.

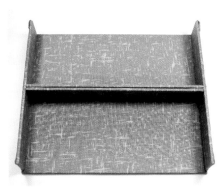

11. Place the remaining side panel in the gap on the opposite side to the first and join to the base, making sure that the 3mm gap before the end of the base is left on the same side as the first side panel. Join the end of the ring holder to the second side panel just on the top edges in the same way as the first side panel.

12. Cut and cover interior front and back panels which are 6mm smaller than the width of the base by the same depth as the sides. Join the back panel to the base and sides at the end without the 3mm gap before the end of the base.

13. The front panel is placed between the two sides so that there is still a 3mm gap left all along the base before the edge of the board. Starting from one side edge, join the front to both side ends and the base.

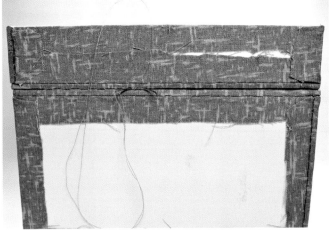

14. Cut and cover an exterior panel with the exterior silk which is the same width as the base by the depth of the side panels. Place this panel along the gap left along the edge of the board and stitch into place on all edges to join the panel to the base and sides as well as the top edge of the interior front.

15. Place the tray tier on top of the cupboard tier and join the base of the tray to the top of the cupboards on all sides. The exterior silk panel on the tray was designed to fit on top of the base in order to keep the top and base join the same as the previous tiers.

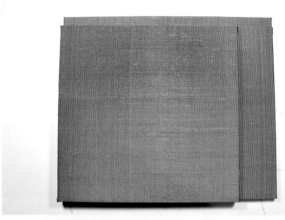

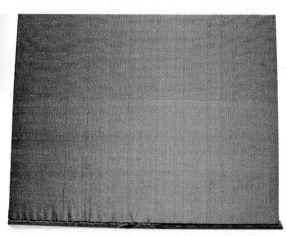

1. Measure the width, depth and height of the constructed tiers. Cut and cover with the contrasting exterior silk fabric two side panels, back and base for the exterior. The base should be cut 6mm wider and 3mm deeper than the constructed tier measurements. The two sides should be cut so they are the same height as the constructed interior tiers and 3mm smaller than the depth of the base. The back should be the same width as the base and the same height as the exterior sides.

2. Place a side and the base panel together with the right side facing out and so that the side sits on top of the wrong side of the base and there is a gap at one end for the back panel to fit into. Join together.

3. Join the back to the joined side and base panels, placing it in the gap left at the end of the side so that the right side is facing outwards.

4. Join the second of the side panels to the base and back in the same way as the first on the opposite side. Both side panels should sit flush with the front of the base.

5. Place the constructed interior tiers into the constructed exterior panels and join the two together along the front three edges only, leaving the top edges unjoined until the lid is ready to be attached to the box.

1. Measure the final width and depth of the constructed box and cut out a panel of board for the lid using those measurements. Cut out a second panel which is 3cm smaller on both sets of sides so that there will be a 1.5cm gap on all edges between the two boards. Using the smaller board, cut out a piece of bump to cover one side of the board.

2. Place the embroidery over the top of the bump; centre the design on the board and lace following the instructions in Chapter 2.

3. Cut out a piece of the exterior silk fabric with a larger allowance of 5cm on each side. Place tape on the edges of the board leaving a gap of 2cm or more between the tape and the edge of the board.

4. Making sure the grain of the fabric is aligned with the edge of the board, stick the edges of the fabric to the tape starting with the two long sides, to make sure they are at a tight tension. Fold and pin half of each corner mitre in place and then fold over the smaller sides to complete each mitre. The reason I have used tape rather than glue is so that the fabric can be adjusted as necessary when folding the mitred corners.

5. Stitch the folds of the mitred corners together making sure they are joined more than 1.5cm from the corners of the board and remove the pins.

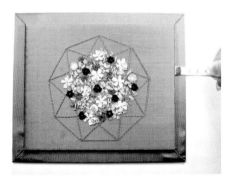

6. Place the mounted embroidery on top of the larger board with the mitred corners facing up. Using a tape measure, check that there is a 1.5cm gap between the edge of the embroidery and the edge of the mitred board on all sides.

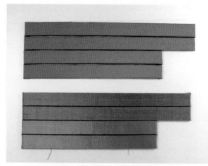

7. Secure the board in place with pins in the corners and stitch the mounted embroidery to the mitred board along all edges.

8. Using the measurements of the larger board and a depth measurement of 1.5 cm on all panels, cut and cover exterior front and back panels the same length as the large board, and side panels 6mm smaller than the width of the larger board. Then cut and cover interior front and back panels 6mm smaller than the exterior front and back panels, and two side panels 6mm smaller than the exterior side panels.

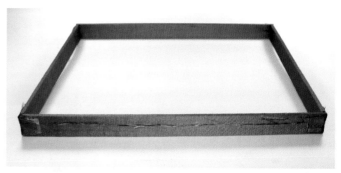

9. Join the two interior side panels to each end of the interior back panel so that the side panels sit on top of the right side of the back panel.

10. Join the interior front panel onto the ends of the side panels so that a rectangle is constructed from the panels with the right side of the fabric facing inwards.

11. Join the two exterior side panels, right side facing outwards, to each end of the exterior back panel so that the side panels sit on top of the wrong side of the back panel.

12. Join the exterior front panel to the end of one of the side panels with the right side of the fabric facing outwards, leaving the final corner unjoined.

13. Wrap the exterior panels around the interior panels to make sure that they fit together perfectly and join the final corners of the exterior panels together.

14. Cut a length of ribbon for a support each side of the lid and separate the interior and exterior lid sections. Using double-sided tape, attach the ribbon at a 35°–45° degree angle to the wrong side of the exterior side panels near the back edge of the lid. This should be measured so that the outside edge of the ribbon is approximately 5cm from the back panels on both side panels.

15. Place the interior lid sections within the exterior lid sections again, taking care not to move the ribbon. Starting the thread just before one of the ribbon supports, join the interior and exterior lid panels together, stitching through both lengths of ribbon to secure them and working around all edges of the lid.

16. Flip the joined lid sections over and join together the other sides of the panels on all sides.

17. Place the top part of the lid onto the base panels and join together, working along all sides.

1. Join the back exterior panel of the box to the interior back panel of the tray starting along the side less than 5cm from the back panel and stopping less than 5cm along the opposite side panel and leaving the end of the thread unfinished. The ribbon supports will be joined between the interior and exterior side panels at the end of each 5cm joined section.

2. Place the lid on top of the box and, using the ladder holding stitch, secure the lid to the back edge of the box.

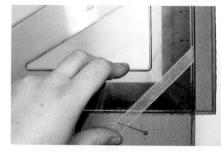

3. Placing a set square on the top edge of the side of the box with the unfinished thread, pull the lid up to the other edge of the set square and then pull the ribbon taut following the angle that it will be secured in. Place a pin 1cm from the top edge of the box.

4. Trim the ribbon 5mm from the pin and place a small piece of double-sided tape on the end of the ribbon.

5. Sticking the other side of the tape to a mellor, push the end of the ribbon down between the interior and exterior sides so that the lid sits at a right angle to the main box.

6. Taking up the unfinished thread, continue stitching together the interior and exterior sides until you reach the already joined front sections, passing the thread through the ribbon to secure it to the box. The mellor can be removed when a few securing stitches are holding the ribbon in place.

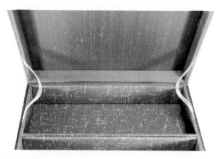

7. Repeat steps 3–6 on the opposite side of the box to join the other lid support to the box. All interior and exterior box panels should now be joined together.

1. Check the internal height and width measurements of the cupboard spaces and cut out two panels 1mm smaller on the height and width than the internal space for each cupboard door. Clamp to a table one pair at a time above a cutting mat.

2. Using a hand drill and a drill bit slightly larger than the bolt, carefully drill a hole through both pieces of board, 1cm in from the edge and centred on the upright edge of the door. This step is repeated for the other pair of doors. The cutting mat is essential to avoid drilling into the table beneath.

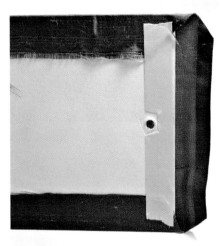

3. Cover one of each pair with the exterior silk fabric. Cut a gap in the tape along the edge with the hole so that it is not covered by the tape.

4. Push a stiletto through the drilled hole to make a hole through the fabric.

5. Cover the interior panels of each set of doors in the same way as the exteriors but using the same silk that was used for the embroidery.

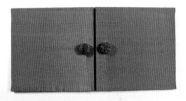

6. Taking one set of doors, line up the holes so that the right sides of each door are facing outwards, and pass the bolt of the handle through the hole from the interior side; attach the handle nut to the bolt on the exterior side of the door. Repeat this step with the other pair of doors.

7. Join the interior and exterior parts of the door together on all sides.

8. Place the doors within the opening of the cupboards so that the handles are both nearest the centre support of the box. Join the exterior door edge to the interior cupboard side to create a hinge for each door.

CHAPTER 10

DESIGNING YOUR OWN BOXES

lanning and designing a hand-crafted box to store a special keepsake or precious items can be very satisfying. Adorning the box with embroidery can be very rewarding, and once completed it will be entirely your own creation and will perfectly fit the item(s) you have planned to store within it. This can be a very challenging task: the box construction itself can be quite complicated, and the embroidery you have chosen to mount on the box may be designed specifically with the shape of the box, design of the items or person who the box is for in mind.

When planning a box there are several aspects to consider:

1. What will be stored within the box? Will there be small items that need dividers? Will you need to increase space later for more items? Start by laying the item(s) on a table and measuring them to work out the minimum size that the interior of the box needs to be. Add an allowance of between 5mm and 2cm to ensure a good fit and ease of removal once the box is completed. The number of items will also determine whether an additional tray is required, if dividers are needed and how big they will need to be. Might stacking trays be more appropriate?

2. What shape is best suited to the items you wish to keep in the box? Rectangular, square, circular, multi-sided? For a tiara, for example, you would want the box to be circular; for a tie clip and cuff links you would require a rectangular box. If you have various small tools that you wish to keep together then an etui box with six or more sides might be the most practical shape of box, rather than a square one.

3. What embroidery is being mounted and where? On the lid, the sides or even the inside? If the embroidery for the box has already been completed or is a kit you have purchased then the shape of the design will need to be taken into account when deciding on the shape of the box, to avoid having too big a border on one edge. It may be that this works with the design but it is still worth planning around.

4. How thick is the fabric? Is padding required on the exterior and/or interior? Does the fabric require calico backing before embroidering? The thickness of the fabric you wish to use will also have a bearing on the style of the box and the lid. As explained previously, there are some restrictions on the thickness of fabric for some styles of box, since thicker fabric requires a greater allowance and can affect the final look when the panels are joined together. Thin and delicate fabrics may need to be backed with calico before the design can be embroidered; this can be trimmed back when mounting but only to the edge of the back of the card; this can still add to the thickness of the fabric so will need to be taken into account when you are working out the sizes of panels.

Close-up of the Canadian smocking on the chest box from Chapter 7.

5. Where is the box going to be kept? Is the space limited in any way? Is the box going to be kept on a shelf, chest of drawers or in a cabinet? This will all help with determining the size of the box after taking into account the size of the items to be stored within. Boxes have an interior and exterior layer of card so the thickness of the card along with any other added elements will need to be taken into account when working out the final size of the box. If the area in which you are keeping the box has a limited height then a drawer or cupboard may be more appropriate. Will these need handles? If so, do you use beads or screw handles? You will need to think about their placement and when to make holes in the card for the handles to be fixed to or through the card panels.

6. Who is the box for? Is it a gift? How much time do you have available for making the box? Is there a deadline? If the box is a gift or for yourself you may wish the embroidery to contain a monogram, and the design can also determine the shape of the box. If you have a limited amount of time or there is a deadline for a gift then try not to be too ambitious in terms of design;

do not include the more advance elements such as a lock unless it is a necessary design element connected to the theme of the box, such as the *Alice in Wonderland*-themed box in Chapter 7. It is worth bearing in mind that small boxes can be just as time-consuming to make as larger boxes, depending on their complexity – and small panels can be more fiddly to cover than larger ones – but in general, smaller boxes will be quicker to make than larger ones. It is possible to make changes as you go to save time if need be but it is better to plan the box out fully as you are less likely to make mistakes which can cost you time.

7. Is the item valuable and is a lock or mirror required? If so, this will take additional planning. Try to use as little card as possible in your design; it is expensive, and will add to the weight of the box. This is particularly important to consider when the lock or mirror is mounted on a door or lid where it may be hanging unsupported; it therefore needs to be as light as possible to avoid damage. The position of the lock will also have a bearing on the design of your box: if the lock is internal then you will need to consider where the

lock catch will fit into to secure the lid in place. If the lock is exterior then, depending on its style, the size and construction of the casing and keep will need to be planned out and carefully measured to make sure that none of the internal elements of the lock other than the keyhole are visible; does the keyhole have a cover or does it need to be embroidered with buttonhole stitch? When using a mirror, you would ideally want the edges to be hidden in order to avoid catching things on any sharp edges or chips in the glass. The lid or panel might be thicker because of this, if not using a chest lid, so the thickness will need to be taken into account when planning the height of your box and order of construction. You will achieve a better finish if you hide the mirror's edges behind a panel of card.

The answers to these questions will determine the size, style and shape of box you design and what materials you use, along with any of the more advanced elements of construction. This will also determine how much and how many different fabrics you will need along with any other materials such as felt, threads and ribbons or beads.

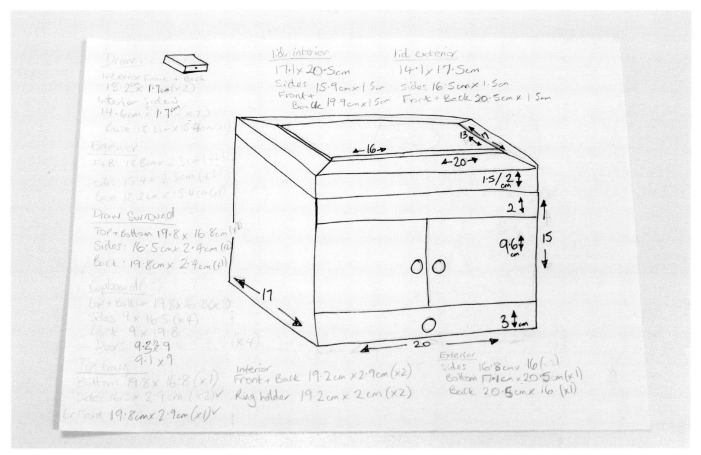

Box construction plan for large jewellery box; it is best to keep the measurements in pencil so they can be changed when necessary.

CONSTRUCTION PLAN

Just as when planning embroidery, a diagram of the desired box is essential when planning out the construction of your box. This can be a rough line drawing with the minimum internal measurements marked on the height, width and depth, or a more detailed drawing giving more estimated measurements of all layers of construction; it really depends on how you work best. If you are a beginner, just complete a rough line drawing of all elements, including separate trays, and start with the internal measurements. As the boxes are worked from the inside out and the measurements can vary depending on materials it is not necessary to create a very detailed drawing with full measurements. I often create a list as I go, working around the diagram, labelling each stage of the construction process in order to keep a record of the panel measurements, in case they are needed at a later date. This is particularly important when making a stacking box, as it may be some time before you need to add an extra layer.

Unlike when you are designing embroidery, a colour plan is not necessary, unless you are planning to use a lot of different colours. Boxes will usually use two colours of fabric: one for the internal panels and another for the exterior, either contrasting or complementary colours. The number of colours you use is entirely up to you but if you are planning to use more than two or three it would be helpful to plan out the colours on one of the design photocopies to make sure that you are not overdoing the number of colours. The number you choose is also likely to be determined by the colour theme of your embroidery. One thing I would avoid is using more than one patterned fabric; it is less visually distracting to have one pattern mixed with plain fabrics than to have several patterned fabrics together. Usually a plain fabric is used on the interior but this really depends on the use and embroidery.

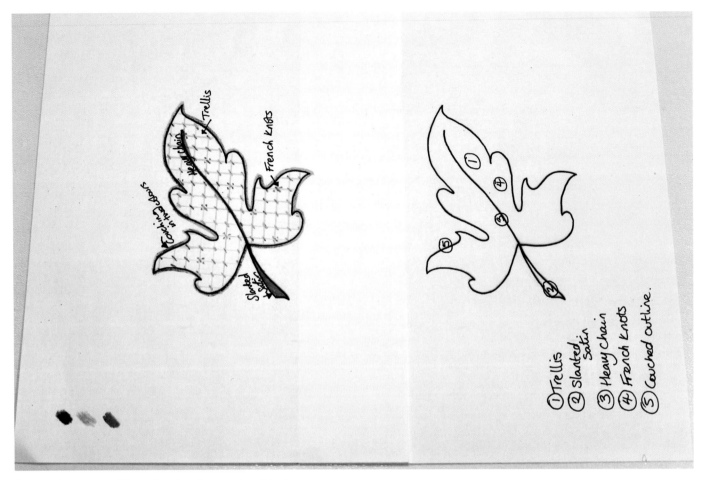

Stitch, colour and working order plans for crewelwork leaf.

STITCH PLAN FOR THE EMBROIDERY

If you are designing your own embroidery for the box you should also create a stitch plan for the design you will be working. This will give details of stitches you wish to use and where they will be worked within the design. Start with a line drawing of the design, which is then photocopied for creating stitch plans, colour plans and in some cases a working order, such as with silk shading. A stitch plan shows where each stitch is to be worked within the design; a colour plan details where each colour will be worked which can help with finding the correct balance of col-

ours. A working order is a useful way of working out which stitches or area needs to be worked first; if your design has a clear depth it is important to work the areas which you wish to be in the background first and then work towards those in the foreground. It is important that all the correct plans are created before you start working on embroidery because the time it takes to work the piece may mean it is left for a while between stitching sessions and a plan means you can continue where you left off without having to remember what your original plan was. That doesn't mean that it can't change as you work the design but it is always useful to have a starting point, especially if the piece involves using a lot of different stitches and colours. The

plans do not need to be perfect – a rough plan with a key for stitches and colours combined is fine.

Once the plans are complete you can then work out what and how much material you will need. It is always better to have more of each than you think, as any leftover materials can be incorporated into another design. Extra materials also allow for you to adjust the design as you work if you feel that more is needed to complete the design. Also allow extra fabric around the design, not just to make it easier to achieve the correct tension if using a ring frame but also in case the measurements of the box change more than you think.

GENERAL ORDER OF WORK

Once all of the plans you require have been completed and you have all the materials needed for the box, the embroidery does not need to be completed first, if it is only being mounted on the lid, so it is not essential to have all the materials before starting work on the box. If the embroidery is also on the sides, drawer front or cupboard doors then the embroidery should be worked first. It is useful at this point to make a list of the first panels you need to cut out with the exact measurements. This working order is only a guide; it cannot be set in stone as it does vary depending on the design of your box, but the more boxes you make the better you will understand the way they are constructed and can therefore adapt the process to your own designs.

- If the box has a drawer, internal tray, false bottom supports or dividers, then these will be the panels you need to cut out first, starting with all of the interior panels.
- The interior panels are then covered in the desired fabric and joined together. This is typically done by joining two sides together first, attaching them to the base, and then joining the remaining sides. All right sides will be in the centre of the box or drawer; if you are constructing a drawer and using screw handles then a hole will need to be made in the interior drawer front before it is

covered. If there is a false bottom, the supports will need to be joined to the interior panels before they are all joined together.

- The interior section is then measured and the exterior panel measurements are worked out from these allowing extra for fabric thickness. If a lock is included, such as a box lock, a section to hold one part of the lock might need to be constructed to fit in between the interior and exterior panels.
- The exterior side panels are cut and covered in the desired fabric and joined together. The sides are usually all joined together in one long section and then wrapped around the interior before the last seam is joined; right sides are facing outwards so that the wrong sides are placed together. If you are making a drawer then a handle may need to be added, depending on what style you choose, either to the exterior front before it is joined to the interior if you are using large beads or afterwards if it is a screw type; this will need to line up with the hole in the interior front panel and be created prior to covering with fabric.
- The base of the box is then measured to check the sizing for the exterior base, which is then cut, covered and joined to the bottom of the box.
- If you are making a drawer the casing for the drawer is then constructed leaving a small allowance to allow the drawer to slide out easily; the interior is constructed first.

- Measure the top of the box to work out the measurements of the lid. Then, depending on the style of the lid, it can either be partly constructed up to the point where the mounted embroidery is attached to the rest of the lid or you can start the embroidery and leave constructing the lid until the embroidery is completed. If a mirror or lock is added to the lid, any supporting panels will need to be added during the interior lid construction.
- The embroidery for the lid can then be worked following your plans. If the measurements for the box have changed drastically, and you have designed the embroidery not to have a border around it, then it is worth working out the measurements for the top and cutting the panel of card to hold behind your design. This is so you can decide whether to have a border or increase the size of the design before transferring the design onto the fabric.
- The embroidery is then mounted onto the exterior top panel and joined to the rest of the lid. The lid hinge is then created if there is one and if there are doors on the box these can then be measured (leaving a small allowance for ease of movement), cut, covered and attached to the box. Any handles will need to be attached to the doors during construction; when this is done will depend on the style of the handles.

STITCH GLOSSARY

Buttonhole stitch

Start with the thread at the back of the fabric edge to be worked. Loop the thread from the back to the front of the fabric and hold in a loop, take the needle down into the fabric away from the edge and carry the needle behind the fabric and up into the loop. Pull the thread tight so that a straight stitch is created with the end of the thread holding the stitch in place.

Closed loop pendant couching

Secure the end of the couching thread with a couple of stitches close together; twist the thread being couched into a loop. Bring the needle up inside the loop close to the cross-over point, stitch over and down the other side of where the threads cross over and continue to create another loop with a small gap between it and the first loop. A mellor can be used to help achieve evenly sized loops.

Couching

Lay the threads to be couched on top of the design line and secure in place with two stitches close together leaving a tail of at least an inch. Continue to stitch small straight stitches at a 90° angle to the couched thread with the stitches placed 4–5mm apart.

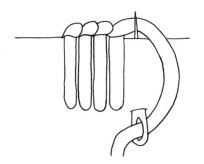

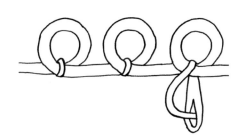

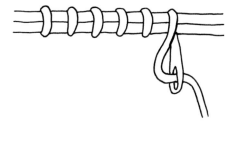

Cutwork over string padding

1. Cut the metal threads to size and starting from the centre of the shape to be worked, thread the metal thread onto a double waxed thread like a bead. Stitch over the padding angling the needle as close as possible to the padding. When working up the design, stitches should be worked from top to bottom, tucking the needle close to the previous metal thread.

2. When working down the design the stitch should be worked from bottom to top, again tucking the needle in close to the previous metal thread to avoid gaps and to help create the 'S' shape.

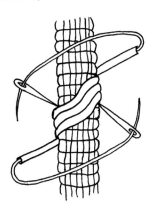

Detached chain

1. Bring the thread to the front of the fabric; stitch down in the same hole or near to the end of the thread to create a loose loop.

2. Carry the needle at the back of the fabric and bring the needle up about 5–6mm away so that the needle is inside the loop; pull the thread to tighten the loop against it. Carrying the needle over the loop, stitch down just next to where the thread came up, trapping the loop against the fabric.

Florentine stitch

This stitch is worked over four threads of the canvas but the placement of the stitches varies depending on the design being worked. While still worked across four threads the next stitch can be carried down by 1–4 threads. The stitches should be worked such that the thread travels the shortest distance across the back of the canvas.

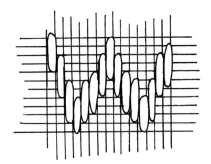

French knots

With the thread on the top of the fabric, wrap the thread once over the needle; pass half the needle through the fabric next to the end of the thread; pull the knot tight and then pull the rest of the needle through to the back securing the knot in place.

Heavy chain

1. Start with a detached chain with a slightly longer holding stitch over the loop. Bring the thread up just under the start of the first loop and pass the needle under the holding stitch for the first loop.

2. The next loop starts just under the second loop with the needle being passed under both of the previous loops.

3. The next and following stitches are started in the same way as before but the needle is passed between the starting points of the loops so that the loop length remains the same throughout.

Herringbone stitch

1. Starting with the thread near the edge of the panel or bottom of the design area, take the needle up through A. Take the needle down at B, about 1 cm upwards in a diagonal direction from A. Carry the needle under the fabric to C so it is almost in line with point A.

2. Start the next stitch by carrying the thread over the fabric and taking the needle down through the fabric at point D and working the stitch back towards point E. Continue by alternating between steps one and two until you reach the end of the area to be worked.

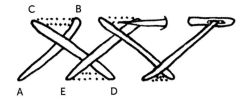

Honeycomb darning stitch

This counted stitch is worked in horizontal rows across three threads of the fabric, with the horizontal stitches carried under three threads and then carried vertically over three threads. When reaching the end of a row the stitch is carried over two threads, under two and then back over two threads before continuing to work the stitch back in the other direction. The threads should meet where the thread is carried under in the middle of the stitches. Try to fit the pattern all the way to the edges of the design where possible even if only part of the stitch can be completed.

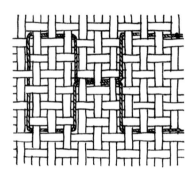

Iris stitch

Start with a detached chain, bring the needle up underneath and to one side of the chain, pass the needle under the chain to form a fly-like stitch. The stitch is finished with a French knot in a different colour in the centre of the chain.

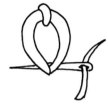 

Long and short stitch

1. Worked over a split stitch edge; the first row of single strand stitches are worked from the inside of the design area over the top of the split stitch and tucked tightly against the outside edge. The stitch length should be varied between short, medium and long, and no stitches the same length should sit next to each other.

2. For the second row the stitches should split the ends of those in the previous row and be carried down into the design area. The starting position should vary based on the length of the stitch it is splitting and again the length of each stitch should vary. This is continued in rows that should not be visible once the design area has been filled; the colours of the threads in each row can be mixed rather than the same colour to create a 'painted' effect.

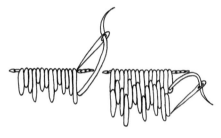

Padded satin

1. Work a split stitch around the edge of the design and then using a thick thread (coton floche) for the padding stitch a small horizontal stitch in the centre of the shape followed by slightly longer vertical stitches worked over the top of the first.

2. More horizontal stitches are worked over the top of the vertical stitches filling in the gaps to the inside edge of the split stitch. More layers should be worked for larger areas but the final layer must be in the opposite direction to the desired direction of the top layer to avoid the stitches sinking.

3. Using a stranded cotton, work the vertical stitches over the padding from the outside edge of the split stitch, tucking the needle down over the outside edge of the opposite split stitch edge to form a neat edge around the shape until all of the shape has been filled.

Pearl purl

Stretch the pearl purl slightly (or overstretch if using stranded cotton); with a single waxed thread secure the end with a whole twist on top with two stitches between the first two pearls. Bring the needle up at the bottom of the gap between the pearls and stitch down at the top of the gap between the pearls so that when pulled through the thread is hidden in the gap between the pearls. Continue stitching the small back stitches every 3–4 twists of the pearls. The end should be cut so that a whole pearl is visible and again secured with two stitches in the same gap before securing the thread to the fabric.

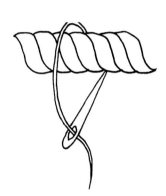

Plunging

Couched threads are plunged close to the securing stitches; thread a large needle with a lasso of sewing thread, pass the needle through the fabric where the couched thread will end. Pass the end of one of the couched threads through the lasso, place a finger either side of the needle to brace the fabric and pull the needle and lassoed thread through to the back of the fabric. Repeat with the other couched thread and then secure both to the back of the fabric by folding back in the direction of the couched stitches and oversewing with sewing thread 1cm of the couched threads before cutting off the excess and securing the sewing thread to the fabric.

Ribbon stitch

With a knot on the back bring the ribbon to the front of the fabric; place a mellor about 1cm away from the start of the ribbon to hold it flat against the fabric. Stitch down through the ribbon on the other side of the mellor and pull through creating a loop over the mellor. Remove the mellor and pull down slightly on the ribbon to create a slightly smaller loop. Continue to work more stitches until you have the desired number of petals.

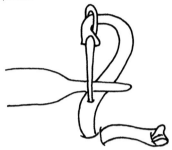

Round gather

1. Cut a small piece of ribbon (4–5cm) and stitch a running stitch along one edge away from the fabric. Once the running stitch is complete, take the needle back to the knot and pass through the ribbon to create a loop.

2. Gather the ribbon before stitching to the fabric and securing with a spangle stitched down with three small stitches.

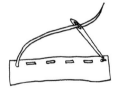

Single fly stitch

Bring the needle up at A and stitch down about 5mm away at B without pulling the thread through. Carry the needle under the fabric bringing the needle up at C (halfway between A and B and about 5mm below them) with the thread looped under the needle. Pull the remaining thread through to form a V shape and then take the needle down at D to form a Y shape. Continue until you have the required number of single fly stitches.

Slanted satin

Start with a split stitch outline all the way around the area to be filled. Starting in the middle and working out to each side of the shape, the straight stitches are worked at a 45° angle from one outside edge of the split stitch carrying the thread across to the opposite edge. Angle the needle slightly so that the stitches sit tightly against the split stitch edge.

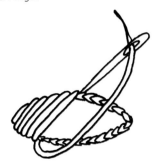

Split stitch

Starting with a small stitch about 2mm long, bring the needle up from the back of the fabric about ⅓ in from the end of the previous stitch 'splitting' the previous stitch and stitch down through the fabric again forming another small stitch about 2mm long. Continue splitting the stitches all the way along the design line until the length to be stitched is complete.

Stem stitch

Start with a straight stitch, about 5–8mm long, along the line to be worked but leave a small loop to the left side of the line. Bring the needle up halfway along the first stitch without catching the thread, then pull the loop tight. Then stitch down about half a stitch length away from the end of the first stitch, leaving the stitch loose by holding the loop to the left side again. For the next and each stitch after; bring the needle up in the end of the stitch under the loop of the previous stitch, pull the loop tight and stitch down a half-stitch from the end of the pre-vious stitch leaving a loop and continue until the end of the line being worked. To finish you can stitch a half-stitch from the middle of the previous stitch and down into the end of the previous stitch to keep continuity of the twisted pattern.

Straight stitch flowers

Straight stitches worked from the outside edge of the flower to be worked; bring the needle up from the back on the outside edge and then down into the centre of the flower, continue until you have the desired number of petals.

String padding

Cut lengths of string slightly longer than the area to be padded; remember that once the string is waxed and stitched it will shrink down slightly. Wax the string. Lay the string along the area, oversew with waxed sewing thread, starting in the centre of the area, angling the needle to pull it in tightly. The strings can be gradually cut in pairs or threes from the bottom layer first in order to taper the padding until the final string is cut and secured in place with two stitches worked from the end and over the top of the previous stitch so they are at 90° to the previous stitches.

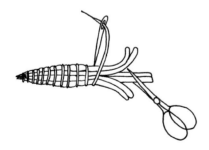

Tall gather

The ribbon is gathered in the centre with a thread attached to the fabric and then stitched down next to where the thread started to gather the ribbon into a small flower, secure with a holding stitch.

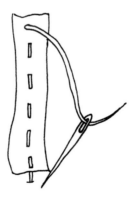

Trailing

Using the desired number of strands or coton floche, lay the thread to be trailed along the design line. Starting from the centre out, stitch at 90° over the laid thread with a single strand, angling the needle as you stitch in order to pull the laid threads tightly together. Continue working the stitches tightly together so the laid thread is hidden beneath. The number of laid threads can be reduced to taper the thickness of the line by gradually cutting away strands of the laid thread from the bottom strands first until the desired thickness is reached, making sure that all ends are stitched over at the end of the design line.

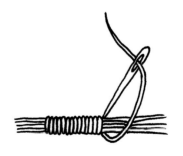

Wave stitch filling

This counted stitch is worked in horizontal rows across four and two threads of the fabric, with the horizontal stitches carried under four threads. The thread is then carried vertically over four threads and across two threads so that the thread is taken down halfway between the horizontal thread carried under the threads of the linen. When reaching the end of a row the stitch is carried under one thread, over two and then back under three threads to where the previous row finished before continuing to work the stitch back in the other direction. The threads should meet where the thread is carried under in the middle of the stitches; try to fit the pattern all the way to the edges of the design where possible even if only part of the stitch can be completed.

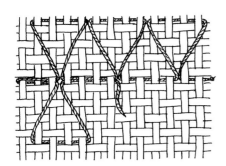

Whipped backstitch

Start by working a back stitch (start the first stitch a stitch length in from the end of the design line, 3–4mm, and stitch back down at the start. Continue stitching a stitch length away from the previous stitch and then back into the end of the previous stitch). Start a different coloured thread at the beginning of the back stitch and work back along the back stitches by passing the needle from the top to bottom under each stitch to create a twisted cord like effect.

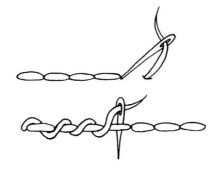

Woven wheel in ribbonwork

1. Draw a circle on the fabric in pencil, working from the centre out to just beyond the pencil line, using stranded cotton stitch five bars spaced evenly around the circle. Using a long length of ribbon, starting with a knot on the top just outside the circle, the needle is brought up in the centre to one side of one of the bars using a chenille needle, which is then passed eye first under the first bar.

2. The next bar is skipped and the needle taken underneath the next bar. Alternate weaving over and under the bars, working your way around the circle until you cannot fit in any more; you are likely to fit more wraps in than you think to make a really tight rose. The ends of the ribbon are secured on the back behind the completed rose; knots can be left at the back depending on the design and mounting method.

GLOSSARY

Blackwork Black thread worked on white fabric, usually linen, in a variety of counted stitches which can be shaded with different thicknesses of threads.

Calico A cotton fabric that is available in a variety of weights, usually used as a backing for lighter fabrics and also to cover card when mounting.

Canvas work Counted stitches worked on canvas to cover the threads of the canvas, usually worked in wool or thick threads.

Chenille needle A large, sharp needle used for thick threads and ribbon due to its large eye, which prevents damage to the threads.

Colourfast Colourfast threads and fabrics should not lose dye when washed. Most modern fabrics are colourfast but it is always worth checking with a colour test.

Colour plan A guide produced prior to starting an embroidery project to show where the colours you will be employing are to be used, this can help achieve a balanced design before you start stitching avoiding unpicking work.

Colour test A process of checking whether threads and fabrics are colourfast. Instructions can be found in Chapter 1.

Conservation card Solid or cotton core acid-free mountcard, available in a variety of thicknesses. This is the recommended card to use for box-making because of its strength and durability.

Construction plan A guide produced prior to starting the construction of a box with rough measurements and design details, such as dividers, trays, tiers and so on.

Couching The method of stitching laid threads onto a fabric by stitching over them with a separate thread.

Crewel needle/embroidery needle Sharp needles in various sizes with an oval-shaped eye for use with wool, stranded cotton and other embroidery threads.

Crewelwork Embroidery traditionally worked in wool threads on a linen twill fabric.

Curved needle A needle which has been curved during the manufacturing process in order to make joining two edges together easier.

Cutwork A form of goldwork where the metal threads are cut, threaded onto a needle and stitched over string padding.

Daylight bulb A lightbulb that emits a white light to emulate daylight so that fabric and threads appear in their true colour rather than being changed by a yellow light as emitted by standard bulbs.

Design transfer   The method of transferring a design onto fabric: prick and pounce, light box or tissue paper and tacking.

Embroidery and fabric scissors Embroidery scissors are small, fine scissors to provide greater accuracy for cutting threads; a separate pair should be kept purely for goldwork. Fabric scissors are larger scissors for cutting larger areas of fabric quickly and should not be used for cutting paper or other non-fabric materials as it will blunt them.

Embroidery hoop   Two wooden hoops used to sandwich the fabric together to keep it and the stitches at the correct tension throughout the embroidery process.

Embroidery stitches   General stitches that are not specific to one technique and can be used across a range of techniques or as general surface stitches.

Godet   A triangular piece of fabric inserted between the sides on an etui box and used to create a larger tray area for keeping tools in one place while stitching.

Goldwork   The use of various metal threads to create impressive raised embroidery; specialist techniques are used which can take some time to master. It can also be combined with other techniques such as stumpwork, silk shading and ribbonwork.

Kid leather   A soft, thin leather which is perfect for use on exterior sides of boxes and lids with larger panels to cover due to the method used to secure the leather to the card.

Ladder stitch   A stitch used in box-making to join the panels together invisibly by creating a ladder between the two panels.

Leather appliqué   Another form of goldwork using metallic coloured leather to create a shape which is then surrounded by pearl purl; it can also be stitched on using other techniques such as cutwork.

Lightbox/pad   A box or pad containing a light in order to transfer a design onto fabric. The light shines through the paper and fabric highlighting the design lines, which can then be traced with a fabric pencil or pen.

Linen   A natural fabric that has large threads and an open weave which is perfect for counted thread techniques (blackwork, whitework) and techniques using thicker threads (crewelwork, ribbonwork). Available in various weaves including twill weave and even weave, as well as in various TPI (threads per inch) sizes.

Mellor   A flat metal tool usually used for goldwork but also used in other techniques to help protect fabrics and materials from being damaged when laid or removed.

Mitre   A technique used during mounting and in box-making to fold a visible corner into a neat diagonal line to the corner point, which is sewn into place with ladder stitch.

Padding felt or bump   Used to create a padded, even surface for an embroidery to sit on or used to create a protective section inside a box. It is also used in goldwork along with string padding for cutwork.

Plunging   The method used to finish off couched threads, either goldwork or embroidery threads, by using a large needle with a lasso to take the threads to the back of the fabric where they can be secured in place.

Propelling pencil   A technical pencil with a fine lead is ideal for drawing the cutting line on the card because the line thickness remains the same throughout and does not smudge.

Ribbon embroidery   A form of embroidery using specialist and embroidery stitches with silk ribbon rather than cotton threads.

Sewing thread   A polyester sewing thread usually used in sewing machines; used to join panels together in box-making because it is fine, durable and stronger than stranded cotton.

Silk shading   A form of embroidery using long and short stitches in various colours of thread to paint a realistic picture of the subject.

Smocking   A method of using stitches to gather the fabric into pleats, which form a repeated pattern.

Spangles   Small round flat metal sequins used in goldwork and ribbonwork.

Stiletto   A metal tool with a tapered point used for making holes in fabric without damaging the threads; traditionally used for making eyelets and can also be used to make holes in card for handles.

Stitch plan   A plan of the design showing where each stitch is to be worked, or used to create a working order where the same stitch is used throughout.

Stranded cotton   A general embroidery thread made up of six strands twisted together, which can be used separately or in various numbers worked together.

Stumpwork embroidery   A form of raised embroidery creating a 3D effect using wired pieces, padding and beadwork.

Tacking   Usually a running stitch which is used to temporarily mark an area of the fabric, transfer a design or hold pieces of fabric together; it is removed once the embroidery or another method has been completed.

Tapestry needle   A blunt needle with a long eye which is used in counted techniques such as blackwork, whitework and canvas work to stitch between threads of the fabric without splitting or damaging them.

TPI (threads per inch)   This is the standard measurement for gauging the fineness of a fabric, so a 32TPI means the fabric has 32 threads per inch of fabric.

Whitework   White threads traditionally worked on white even-weave linen in a variety of techniques, including pulled work, drawn threads, counted stitches, Mountmellick, monograms, shadowwork, broderie anglaise and Hardanger.

··ᘒ[ACKNOWLEDGEMENTS]ᘒ··

For her unwavering encouragement I really owe everything to my mum. Even though she is no longer here, my memories of her have remained with me throughout the process of writing this book, encouraging me to achieve more than I thought possible. When I was growing up she taught me a lot of different craft skills and it was she who found out about and encouraged me to apply to the Royal School of Needlework Apprenticeship – twice, after narrowly missing out the first time (only six places were available before the degree programme replaced it).

My time at the RSN was one of the hardest but most rewarding experiences of my life. I am so glad that I did not give up – even after several 2am stitching sessions – because none of this would have been possible without the skills I learned during my three years there. I hope that with this book more opportunities will open up to return to a place that is very close to my

heart; I miss walking through the corridors of Hampton Court Palace and talking to others who are as passionate about my craft as I am. I am also grateful for my time spent at the University of the Creative Arts studying for my degree; while there I learned a completely different set of skills and the experience has helped shape me into who I am today, giving me the confidence to think writing a book was possible.

Lastly, but most importantly, I need to thank my husband and son for their support and encouragement in writing this book. My husband supported me financially during the final years of my apprenticeship and during my degree, and when I first mentioned the idea for this book, something I had been thinking about for a while, he told me to just go for it and I am so glad I did. After the many cups of coffee while hidden away in my office at the weekends to keep to my deadlines, repeatedly underestimating how long things will take to complete, I feel privi-

leged that we are now in a position to turn my passion for embroidery and craft into a career while bringing up our family. This really is proof that, no matter what your dream is, you should never be afraid to try today, because you never know what could happen tomorrow.

Emma Broughton.

··⚜[FURTHER READING]⚜··

Barnden, B. *The Embroidery Stitch Bible*. Search Press, 2003.

Cox, S. *RSN Essential Stitch Guides: Bead Embroidery*. Search Press, 2013.

Davies, O. and Holdsworth, G. *Embroidered Knot Gardens: Using Three-Dimensional Stumpwork, Canvas Work and Ribbon Work*. Batsford, 2006.

Dier, M. *Thread Painting and Silk Shading Embroidery*. The Crowood Press, 2018.

Doyle, R. *RSN Essential Stitch Guides: Canvaswork*. Search Press, 2013.

Hogg, B. *RSN Essential Stitch Guides: Blackwork*. Search Press, 2010.

Lansberry, L. *RSN Essential Stitch Guides: Whitework*. Search Press, 2012.

Long, S. *Ribbonwork Embroidery*. The Crowood Press, 2017.

McDonald, J. *RSN Essential Stitch Guides: Crewelwork*. Search Press, 2010.

Richman, H. *Stumpwork Embroidery*. The Crowood Press, 2017.

Sinton, K. *RSN Essential Stitch Guides: Stumpwork*. Search Press, 2011.

··⚜[SUPPLIERS]⚜··

*I*f you have any questions regarding equipment or materials used in this book or have problems finding the correct items then please contact the author at ebroughton@live.co.uk. I am also more than happy to answer construction or technique questions should you have any and look forward to seeing your box designs turned into reality.

The Bead Merchant   www.beadmerchant.co.uk
For beads and beading supplies.

Emma Broughton   www.fairywrenembroidery.com
For smaller quantities of card hand-cut from larger boards, smaller quantities of some gold and metal threads, triangular cutting curved needles, even-weave linen, embroidery and box-making kits and equipment.

Closs and Hamblin   www.candh.co.uk
For great quality and a large selection of quilting cottons, threads, needles, cords and ribbons, ring frames, lighting and magnification equipment, and general haberdashery.

Conservation by Design   www.cxdglobal.com
For bulk orders of 5 or more sheets of conservation card, either solid or cotton core, roughly 1120 × 815mm in size only.

Crafty Ribbons   www.craftyribbons.com
For quality silk ribbons in small or large quantities and other ribbon types.

Creative Beadcraft   www.creativebeadcraft.co.uk
For beads and beading supplies.

Creative Quilting   www.creativequilting.co.uk
For a very wide range of quilting cottons, Sewline fabric pencils, and quilting equipment.

Golden Hinde   www.golden-hinde.co.uk
Goldwork materials, mellors and stilettos.

Hobbycraft   www.hobbycraft.co.uk
Lamps, magnification, general haberdashery.

Identity Leather Craft   www.identityleathercraft.com
For great-quality fine leathers that are suitable for box-making; you can use vintage leathers if they are fine enough and in a good condition.

Jaycotts   www.jaycotts.co.uk
For a full range of high-quality professional scissors in various shapes and sizes.

Merchant & Mills   www.merchantandmills.com
For high-quality fabric scissors in various sizes; for cheaper alternatives to mellors and stilettos you could use a bamboo point turner and a tailor's awl.

Sew and So   www.sewandso.co.uk
For both Anchor and DMC brands as well as a wide range of quilting fabrics and other embroidery accessories.

The Silk Route   www.thesilkroute.co.uk
For a wide range of quality silk fabrics suitable for embroidery.

Toye & Co   www.thetoyeshop.com
For larger quantities of all gold and metal threads.

Wilko   www.wilko.com
For unbranded daylight bulbs that can be used in any lamp or ceiling light.

INDEX